Promotions Forecasting:
Forecast Adjustment
Techniques in Software

Shaun
Snapp

Promotions Forecasting: Forecast Adjustment Techniques in Software

For information about this title or to order other books and/or electronic media, contact the publisher:

SCM Focus Press
PO Box 29502 #9059
Las Vegas, NV 89126-9502
http://www.scmfocus.com/scmfocuspress
(408) 657-0249

ISBN: 978-1-939731-46-3

Printed in the United States of America

Contents

CHAPTER 1

Introduction

Promotions are a major focus of sales and marketing. Just about everyone is familiar with seeing promotions in everyday shopping, especially at retail outlets. However, many types of promotions are not visible to consumers. Promotions can take place between parties, or be directed towards an internal sales force or nonretail distribution partners. In fact, from the forecasting and tracking perspective, one of the confusing aspects of promotions is that they can be run in so many different areas, making it difficult to track them and account for them in the forecast.

While promotions lead to real changes in demand, much has been written about how to plan promotions rather than how to account for and forecast promotions so that the promoted item is available to meet the demand. Not only do internal promotions change the demand for a company's products, but competitor promotions do as well! Obviously forecasting promotions is quite important, because accurately accounting for promotions is the only way to guarantee the availability of the promoted product (unless the product is made to order). Insufficient availability of a product to meet demand should count as a service failure and reduce the service level, as would a normal stock out.

A promotion is a change in the terms of the sale of the item. Promotions can be run on old products or new products, but the important distinction of a promotion is that the product or service itself is not what is different—the "promotional difference" is the terms of the sale.

The following are the generally agreed-upon categories of promotions:

1. *Customer Promotions:* The most common type of promotion, these promotions are directed at customers and are what people typically think about when they think of a promotion.

2. *Sales Promotions:* These are promotions directed by the producer to a supply chain partner.

3. *Trade Promotions:* Promotions directed towards a retailer or wholesaler are referred to as trade promotions.

Within each category of promotion, there are different ways of changing the terms of the sale. The most common is a price reduction, and price reductions are the types that are used as examples in this book. However, there are quite a few others, including the following:

1. Loyalty Programs

2. Contests

3. Incentives

4. Buy One Get One Free

5. Free Samples

These types of promotions are referred to as non- price reduction promotions. Some people who study promotions consider non-price reduction promotions to be of more value than price reduction promotions. Non-price reductions are considered to have longer-term effects and do not erode the perceived brand value. Points programs offered by hotel and airline companies might not seem like promotions at first because they are unrelated to the price paid and are not run for a specific period of time, qualities we often attribute to a promotion. However, they are promotions.[1] When a member of a points program cashes in points for a free flight or a free night's stay, this is a cost that the company would not ordinarily incur. When a casino offers "comps" (e.g., complimentary stays, food, drink, access to exclusive amenities at the casino), this is also a

---

[1] The first loyalty/points program in the airline industry was created by American Airlines in the early 1980s. It was tremendously successful, quickly copied by other airlines (although one has to question the effectiveness of a points program in increasing sales if all airlines have the same program) and then loyalty programs of this nature spread to hotels. Now almost every person who travels on a regular basis is part of one or multiple loyalty programs. The degree to which loyalty programs have increased is evidenced by the fact that Starbucks has a "Starbucks Card." This means that a program that started with an expensive item—an airplane ticket—has moved all the way to a coffee house (https://www.starbucks.com/card). Of course, companies do not only offer membership programs to increase sales specifically due to the change in terms provided to the customer, but also to increase sales over the longer term by tracking purchases and being able to mine this data to recognize exploitable relationships. Grocery stores, which make extensive use of retail promotions as well as offering loyalty/discount cards, are probably the best known for doing this, and do it to such a degree that they have received negative press for what amounts to violating their customers' privacy. However, pretty much any company with a loyalty program now does this to some degree. In the 1980s, when American Airlines developed their loyalty program, businesses were very limited in their ability to mine this data, but with the massive increase in computing power combined with the great increase in loyalty programs, loyalty programs have become a major source of marketing intelligence.

promotion. A promotion is any cost that the company incurs to increase sales. The end consumer may see the promotion, or it may be hidden in the form of a sales promotion or trade promotion; unseen promotions occur all the time in the marketplace.

Other common promotions that are not discrete events include loyalty or membership promotions, such as Sam's Club, Costco, Amazon Prime, Zappos VIP membership, and credit card cash-back programs.

As we will see further on in this book, all promotions can be measured for the effect on sales, and the history of any type of promotion can be used to adjust the forecast for future promotions. From the forecasting perspective, the way a promotion is configured is quite important because some types of promotions are easier to track and relationships are easier to observe than others. If a promotion is difficult to track, it is also difficult to forecast.

To the marketer, the type of promotion is part of the overall promotional strategy; however, to the forecasting specialist the only important feature is that the promotion signifies a change in some term or incentive that results in a change in demand. Any change like this can be modeled and then predicted for its effect on future demand. The trick is in creating a database of historical changes, whatever they may be, and then using this database to predict the future changes in demand from the rerunning of these promotions. All promotions forecasting is based upon an implied relationship between the promotional change and how demand will respond to this change.

Generally, promotional forecasting is not a major focus of forecasting books, forecasting classes or statistical forecasting. However, promotions can be an incredibly powerful influence on demand and a major factor in reducing forecast accuracy when unaccounted for in the demand history. I have been an avid reader of forecasting books for some time, and the depth of problems that are caused in forecasting by promotions was not apparent to me until I worked with a number of companies on forecast improvement projects. On these projects, I consistently found that the inability of companies to account for promotions was a major contributor to forecast error. Through my work with these companies, I found that the effect of promotions on forecast error was often underestimated. In companies where promotions are common, forecasting and accounting for promotions deserves significant attention. Promotional forecasting is now one of the main forecasting services I provide to companies to help improve their forecasts, along with better known offerings such as best-fit forecasting, top-down forecasting and forecast benchmarking.

For those who do not work in the guts of marketing or forecasting it can be surprising what a major factor promotion can play in the strategy of a company. Promotions are common in many industries; however, they are most probably prevalent in the retail and consumer package industry. I have assumed that those that are most interested in promotions have purchased this book. But the promotions forecasting approaches and techniques that are explained in this book can be applied to many different types of promotions, literally in any industry. Therefore I will not spend time in this book differentiating promotions between industries. Clearly, promotions play a small role in some industries. The aerospace and defense industry comes to mind; for instance, generally Lockheed Martin does not run promotions on its fighter planes, offering discounts in March of 15 percent, or "buy one, get one free." However, if you can plan promotions in one industry, you can apply the same techniques to other industries. The more important aspect is how traceable the change in demand is to the specific type of promotion and the quality of data that one is working with.

Forecast Accuracy and Demand Shaping

Regardless of exactly how the promotion is implemented, all promotions have a **similar type of impact** on the forecast, and certain strategies work for accounting for promotions in forecasting. It should be understood that promotions never **improve** forecast accuracy. It is not possible for promotions to do this because promotions distort what I refer to as "authentic demand," which is the demand without the promotion.

Some people have proposed that if a promotion is run during a period of low demand, this can create a more stable demand pattern, therefore reducing variability.[2] There is a name for this; it is called "demand shaping." Demand shaping is the process of creating incentives with customers that smooth demand, or eliminating pre-existing incentives such as promotions or end-of-quarter pushes that distort the demand history and make forecasting more difficult to perform.

Demand shaping is a good idea and is a frequent subject of software vendor marketing and discussions at supply chain conferences. In reality, demand shaping is a bit like a unicorn sighting. This would be a promotion with an operational orientation, as it would level manufacturing output (always a good thing) as well as increase the forecastability of the promoted product. However, it is very rare for production or any other operational function to have any influence on promotions. Instead, promotions are controlled by sales/marketing and are designed to help sales/marketing meet their objectives. In every case I have reviewed, promotions have actually increased sales variability.

> *"Most supply chain managers have no influence in the decisions made by marketing and sales managers. Yet the ramifications make their jobs harder and often result in increased demand volatility and uncertainty. For example, at most consumer packaged goods (CPG) companies, these types of 'self-inflicted' demand variations (due to product promotions) are a company's dominant source of demand variation."*
>
> – Demand Shaping with Supply in Mind

Promotions degrade forecast accuracy by increasing the variability of the sales history, creating unexpected spikes in demand, and increasing the work on the part of the demand planner, as well as on the part of many other individuals throughout the supply chain. While this may not seem like a major problem,

---

[2] The economist John Maynard Keynes essentially proposed the same countercyclical policy, but for government spending. The idea was that by increasing government spending as well as easing monetary policy during periods of low demand, and decreasing spending and tightening monetary policy during periods of high demand, the government could smooth out the business cycles. This is one of the most well known strategies in the field of economics. Those that subscribe to this approach are referred to as "Keynesians."

companies generally greatly **understaff** the forecasting area. Therefore, every extra overhead with respect to forecasting tends to lessen the likelihood that the item in question will be accounted for.[3] Furthermore, because of the existence of competitor promotions, it is extremely unlikely that all of the effects of promotions will ever be accounted for in the forecast system. However, the objective is to capture **as much of the promotional effect** as possible.

This book is practitioner-oriented. There are some papers on forecasting promotions that are highly mathematical, a quotation from one of which I have included below:

> *"There is a clear need to take the promotions for the focal item*
> *and potentially for the related item into account when forecasting*
> *demand. Machine learning techniques allow non-linear*
> *relationships. The use of additive combinations of SRIMA models*
> *and neural networks trained with the residuals of the time series*
> *model and the promotional input to forecasting grocery sales. While*
> *these approaches clearly bring flexibility to the functional form of*
> *promotional impact, there are attempts to incorporate managerial*
> *knowledge of promotional impact to guide the search for more*
> *predictive models, for example, fuzzy rules elicited from managers to*
> *set the initial weights of the neural network."*
>
> – SKU Demand

---

[3] Interestingly, when you ask companies – or the executives in companies – if forecasting is important to them they invariably declare that it is. However, the issue is that the investment into forecasting does not match its declared importance. A number of software vendors have made it easier for some executives to rationalize a low level of investment into forecasting by proposing that the software application itself will allow for a limited headcount. Secondly, most companies severely mis-allocate the resources they do apply to forecasting. This is due to numerous factors ranging from the procurement of difficult-to-implement software to not having an effective way of combining multiple forecasts – most notably statistical and sales – or judgment techniques; in order to get the highest possible forecast accuracy for their investment.

Forecasting in the Presence of Promotions

This is not the only paper to take a highly complex approach to promotions forecasting. In fact, all of the papers I found—and there were not that many—took a similar approach to promotions forecasting; that is, they focused on techniques of forecasting the promotion rather than relying upon signals regarding the promotions from sales/marketing. For some reason these papers seem to ignore the fact that the timing and size of the future promotions are available **right within these companies** in the sales/marketing department. Also, these papers seem to imply that the use of complex forecasting methods is necessary because the promotions must be forecasted statistically, as if the promotions are controlled by some third party that the forecasting department has to outguess, when in fact promotions are controlled by either sales or marketing within the same company.

I don't use any big mathematics to manage promotions in my consulting work. And I would question how effective these complex approaches would be as I find it challenging getting companies to implement the comparatively simple approach that I use. It's very easy to create a complex approach in an academic paper, because the academic paper is not subject to testing in an actual business environment. Companies do not have PhDs available to implement the approach and unlike academic environments, companies are not forecasting 50 product location combinations (PLCs), but instead thousands or hundreds of thousands of PLCs. The approach I use is focused on making adjustments to improve promotions forecasting efficiently, because time is a precious commodity in forecasting departments. Essentially I create a causal model, but it is simple (the promotion adjustment calculator is discussed first in Chapter 6: "Accounting for Promotions in Sales History"). It is calculated in a spreadsheet and is an average of previous promotions, although there is nothing to stop a company from using some type of smoothing on the promotion history observations or from excluding some observations. One can make adjustments to the approach that I describe, but it's not wise to make too many changes, particularly if those changes require more time to perform.

Books and Other Publications on Promotions Forecasting

As I do with all my books, I performed a comprehensive literature review before I began writing. One of my favorite quotations about research is from the highly respected RAND Corporation, a "think tank" based in sunny Santa Monica, California. They are located not far from where I grew up. On my lost surfing weekends during high school, I used to walk right by their offices with my friend, at that time having no idea of the institution's historical significance. RAND's *Standards for High Quality Research and Analysis* publication makes the following statement about how its research references other work.

> *"A high-quality study cannot be done in intellectual isolation:*
> *It necessarily builds on and contributes to a body of research*
> *and analysis. The relationships between a given study and*
> *its predecessors should be rich and explicit. The study team's*
> *understanding of past research should be evident in many aspects*
> *of its work, from the way in which the problem is formulated and*
> *approached to the discussion of the findings and their implications.*
> *The team should take particular care to explain the ways in which*
> *its study agrees, disagrees, or otherwise differs importantly from*
> *previous studies. Failure to demonstrate an understanding of*
> *previous research lowers the perceived quality of a study, despite any*
> *other good characteristics it may possess."*

The few books that include promotions forecasting spend only a few pages on the topic. Providing more coverage was something I very much looked forward to doing with this book; these topics are complex and require the significant attention I was able to allocate to them. This is, as of the time of its publishing, the only book on forecasting promotions. Because of this fact, at the time of its publication, this book contains the **most information** available on forecasting promotions. I am very confident that this book can help many companies improve their forecasting of promotions, and I am somewhat surprised that a book like this was not written some time ago.

The Use of Screen Shots in the Book

I consult using some popular and well-known applications, and I've found that companies have often been given the wrong impression of an application's capabilities. As part of my consulting work, I am required to present the results of testing and research about various applications. The research may show that a well-known application is not able to perform some functionality well enough to be used by a company, and point to a lesser-known application where this functionality is easily performed. Because I am routinely in this situation, I am asked to provide evidence of the testing results within applications, and screen shots provide this necessary evidence.

Furthermore, some time ago it became a habit for me to include extensive screen shots in most of my project documentation. A screen shot does not, of course, guarantee that a particular functionality works, but it is the best that can be done in a document format. Everything in this book exists in one application or another, and nothing described in this book is hypothetical.

How Writing Bias Is Controlled at SCM Focus and SCM Focus Press

Bias is a serious problem in the enterprise software field. Large vendors receive uncritical coverage of their products, and large consulting companies recommend the large vendors that have the resources to hire and pay consultants rather than the vendors with the best software for the client's needs.

At SCM Focus, we have yet to financially benefit from a company's decision to buy an application showcased in print, either in a book or on the SCM Focus website. This may change in the future as SCM Focus grows, but we have been writing with a strong viewpoint for years without coming into any conflicts of interest. SCM Focus has the most stringent rules related to controlling bias and restricting commercial influence of any information provider. These "writing rules" are provided in the link below:

   http://www.scmfocus.com/writing-rules/

If other information providers followed these rules, we would be able to learn about software without being required to perform our own research and testing for every topic.

Information about enterprise supply chain planning software can be found on the Internet, but this information is primarily promotional or written at such a high level that none of the important details or limitations of the application are exposed; this is true of books as well. When only one enterprise software application is covered in a book, one will find that the application works perfectly, the application operates as expected and there are no problems during the implementation to bring the application live. This is all quite amazing and quite different from my experience of implementing enterprise software. However, it is very difficult to make a living by providing objective information about enterprise supply chain software, especially as it means being critical at some point. I once remarked to a friend that SCM Focus had very little competition in providing untarnished information on this software category, and he said, "Of course, there is no money in it."

The Approach to the Book

By writing this book, I wanted to help people get exactly the information they need without having to read a lengthy volume. The approach to the book is essentially the same as to my previous books, and in writing this book I followed the same principles.

1. **Be direct and concise.** There is very little theory in this book and the math that I cover is simple. While the mathematics behind the optimization methods for supply and production planning is involved, there are plenty of books that cover this topic. This book is focused on software, and for most users and implementers of the software, the most important thing to understand is conceptually what the software is doing.

2. **Based on project experience.** Nothing in the book is hypothetical; I have worked with it or tested it on an actual project. My project experience has led to my understanding a number of things that are not covered in typical supply planning books. In this book, I pass on this understanding to you.

3. **Saturate the book with graphics.** Roughly two-thirds of a human's sensory input is visual, and books that do not use graphics—especially educational and training books such as this one—can fall short of their purpose. Graphics have also been used consistently and extensively on the SCM Focus website.

Important Terminology

To understand this book, it is necessary to understand the variety of terminology used throughout it. These terms are divided into different categories, which are described below: General Terms, Forecasting Terms, Marketing Terms,

Application Terms, and Forecasting Application Fields/Terms.

General Terms

1. *Sales/Marketing:* Refers to any person who is from the sales side of a company, such as brand managers, marketing managers and other associated persons.

2. *Supply Chain:* The supply chain functions within a company: forecasting, inventory management, production, procurement, etc.

3. *Market Intelligence:* This is the combined knowledge of the marketplace, customers, products, etc., that resides with sales/marketing and which they use to perform forecast adjustments.

Forecasting Terms

1. *PLC:* Product-location combination. Product A at location B is one product location.

2. *Attribute-based Forecasting:* This is the ability to assign PLCs to flexible hierarchies for use in the forecasting system. An attribute is any characteristic of the product or even of the location. Attributes can be used for forecasting functionality, such as top-down forecasting, or they can be navigational and used to efficiently segment the PLC database. Because attribute-based forecasting is its own topic, I do not cover it in this book from a foundational perspective, but I do explain its importance for promotions forecasting by using and showing attributes in the application examples. However, I cover attribute-based forecasting extensively in my first forecasting book, *Supply Chain Forecasting Software*.

3. *Forecastability:* This is an approximate term use to describe the general maximum forecast accuracy that can be expected from statistically forecasting a PLC. The less forecastable a PLC, the less any statistical method can add value by creating a forecast. Forecastability is important in measuring the performance of any forecasting system/approach/method because it places forecast performance within the context of what was hypothetically possible. A high forecast accuracy is not necessarily val-

idation of a system/approach/method because the item forecasted may be simply easy to forecast. A low forecast accuracy is not necessarily a repudiation of a forecasting system/approach/method because the item forecasted may be very difficult to forecast.

4. *Best-fit Procedure:* This is an automated matching of a PLC to the best forecasting method available in the application that is running the procedure. Best fit works on the basis of the history of the PLC. The best-fit procedure is very well known in forecasting. However, probably "best fit" should have been called "limited best fit" or "pretty good fit," because the procedure can only find the best fit from among the forecasting models that are within its database and not the total universe of forecasting models that are actually available to be tested. Often, companies develop custom forecasting models that are superior in some circumstances to the standard models used by forecasting systems. Unfortunately, custom forecasting models cannot be added to a best-fit procedure without coding/customization, and therefore, comparisons between the best fit matching and other forecasting models must be performed outside of the forecasting system.

5. *Stockpiling:* This is the purchasing of product ahead of actual consumption. Stockpiling is actually a general term that often means to procure items significantly in advance of their usage for a variety of reasons, such as in preparation for a lengthy ocean voyage. However, in this book we will be analyzing the more specialized meaning of the term, which is the purchasing of product ahead of actual consumption in response to an incentive.

6. *Overfitting:* There are at least two ways of defining overfitting, both of which are quite interesting. The practical definition of overfitting is when a model or person creates a forecast model that, while good at matching the history of the predicted item, does not work nearly as well in predicting the future. Wikipedia offers a nice definition that is more technical. I don't think I can improve upon this definition and so I have included it here.[4] *"Overfitting generally occurs when a model is excessively complex,*

---

[4] Joannes Vermorel of Lokad brings up some very interesting points regarding overfit-

such as having too many parameters relative to the number of observations. A model which has been overfit will generally have poor predictive performance, as it can exaggerate minor fluctuations in the data. The possibility of overfitting exists because the criterion used for training the model is not the same as the criterion used to judge the efficacy of a model. In particular, a model is typically trained by maximizing its performance on some set of training data. However, its efficacy is determined not by its performance on the training data but by its ability to perform well on unseen data. Overfitting occurs when a model begins to memorize training data rather than learning to generalize from trend." – Wikipedia

7. *(PAC) Promotion Adjustment Calculator:* A tool for consistently adjusting promotions to the forecast by product category based upon history.

8. *Outlier:* An outlier is a data point that diverges from the other observations of which it is a group. Identification of outliers is one of the steps in accounting for promotions.

Marketing Terms

1. *Cannibalization:* Where the increase in sales for one item leads to decreases in sales of another item, through the process of substitution. In marketing, the term "cannibalization" refers to one's reduction of the sales of one's own item in response to one's action in some other area (such as promotions). Sometimes it is used more broadly to mean when the actions of a competing firm reduces one's sales volume. In this book, the term is used this way as well, and specifically to address scenarios where the promotions of a competitor reduce one's sales. Cannibalization has many causes; however, this book is only concerned with cannibalization **in relation to promotional activity**.

---

ting, stating, "There is no work-around for overfitting Modern statistical theories are built on top of this very concept. Overfitting plays a central part in those theories; no matter which way you approach statistics, overfitting is here to stay." Vermorel has a very nice explanation of overfitting, complete with a video, at this link: http://blog.lokad.com/journal/2009/4/22/overfitting-when-accuracy-measure-goes-wrong.html.

Application Terms

I will be using screen shots of a forecasting application called Smoothie, which is developed by Demand Works, to illustrate different observations from testing, so let's go over an explanation of what you will view in these screen shots.

1. *Resultant History:* This is the black line in the user interface of Demand Works Smoothie, the primary application used in this book to explain promotions. The Resultant History is the actual sales history plus any adjustments. It is not the Actual History.

2. *Fitted Forecast:* The red line you will see in the user interface screen shots is the Fitted Forecast. This is the forecast of the model in the past. Many of those who work in forecasting refer to this as the "ex-post" forecast. I consider "Fitted Forecast" to be a better term and, in my view, more intuitively understandable. The Fitted Forecast, when compared to history over time, shows visually how well the forecast used has predicted history or could have predicted history.

3. *Calculated Forecast:* The green line you will see in the user interface screen shots. The Calculated Forecast is produced by the application based on the data that is in the Resultant History. The forecast is always based upon Resultant History, because we want the forecast to work off of history plus adjustments, and not just the history.

4. *Synchronized Forecast:* The blue line you will see in the user interface screen shots. The Synchronized Forecast is the result of a hierarchy of forecasts and adjustment measures.[5]

In addition to graphical elements, there are several terms that I will use and that are calculated by the application, and understanding them is important to understanding the analysis. So let's go over them now.

Forecasting Application Fields/Terms

---

[5] The paper copy of this book is in black and white, and so the colors will not be apparent, although they will be easy to see, especially as there is legend in each screen shot of Smoothie. In the electronic copy of this book, the colors are visible.

1. *Fitted R-Square:* R-Squared is a measure of the predictive power of a forecasting model. Values range from zero to 1. An R-Squared of 1 means that 100 percent of the variability is explained by the model. It is calculated by comparing the sum of the squared deviations of the forecast with the variance of the series itself. The R-Squared is automatically set to zero if the current calculated forecast would be outperformed by the series mean.

2. *Fitted MAPE:* MAPE stands for Mean Absolute Percent Error. It is a statistical measure of fitted forecast accuracy. This is probably the most common forecast error calculation, and I think the most intuitive. As the name implies, it is equal to the average of the absolute percent errors for all periods. The fitted portion indicates that the calculation is the MAPE of the fitted forecast, which is averaged for the entire time series. (As a note, the fitted MAPE is not reliable for a grouping of products. The fitted MAPE is useful when a single PLC is selected).

3. *Fitted RMSE:* RMSE stands for Root Mean Squared Error. This measures variability of the actual sales history versus the forecast. Primarily we will be using this to compare against the Fitted RMSE No Outliers, to show how the forecast accuracy improves when outliers (typically spikes in demand) are removed.

4. *Fitted RMSE No Outliers:* The RMSE with outliers removed. This time-saving statistic does the job of estimating what the forecast error could be without outliers, and automatically identifies all outliers based upon the settings entered into the forecasting application by the user. Therefore, an outlier's distance from the average is controlled by the model setup.

5. *Series Standard Deviation:* Series standard deviation is the standard deviation of all observations (obtained from resultant history and ignoring leading periods with zero demand). Standard deviation is a commonly used measure of variability that measures the variability of forecast relative to the mean.

6. *Series Mean:* Series mean is the average of all observations (obtained

from resultant history and ignoring leading periods with zero demand).[6]

The SCM Focus Site

As I am also the author of the SCM Focus site, http://www.scmfocus.com, the site and the book share a number of concepts and graphics. Furthermore, this book contains many links to articles on the site, which provide more detail on specific subjects. This book provides an explanation of how supply and production planning software works and aims to continue to be a reference after its initial reading. However, if your interest in supply planning software continues to grow, the SCM Focus site is a good resource to which articles are continually added.

The SCM site dedicated specifically to demand planning is
http://www.scmfocus.com/demandplanning

Intended Audience

Very simply, this book is for anyone interested in improving the forecast accuracy of product databases that include promotions. The book will be useful to those who work in supply chain—which I think is the primary market for the book—and those involved in sales and marketing , particularly those sales and marketing individuals who are interested in improving forecasting accuracy.

If you have any questions or comments on the book, please e-mail me at shaunsnapp@scmfocus.com.

Abbreviations

A listing of all abbreviations used throughout this volume is provided at the end of the book.

Corrections

Corrections and updates, as well as reader comments, can be viewed in the

---

[6] Definitions in this section were taken in part from the *Demand Works Smoothie Help Manual.*

comment section of this book's web page. If you have comments or questions, please add them at the following link:

http://www.scmfocus.com/scmfocuspress/promotions-forecasting/

CHAPTER 2

Promotions from Sales/Marketing's Perspective

Promotions are one of the "seven Ps" of marketing (product, price, promotion, place, packaging, positioning and people). Promotions are also part of the study of pricing, and therefore a subcategory of finance. However, promotions come out of the budget for sales and/ or marketing, and therefore are primarily controlled by sales or marketing. Promotions are the primary way companies get customers of another brand to switch to their brand. And as is covered in Chapter 6, "Accounting for Previous Promotions in Sales History," there is some evidence that part of the bump in sales during a promotion is due to permanent brand-switching after the promotion has ended, although the amount very much depends upon the research study and the environment, product type, etc. Essentially, when that does happen, it means that the consumer has a preference for the company's product, but without the promotion, there was insufficient reason to consider trying it.

Promotions are quite high-profile and an approach to marketing products.

In many companies, the sales and marketing departments increasingly view promotions as a major part of the overall strategy. Promotions have greatly increased in their frequency and according to Gartner; roughly 20 percent of the revenue of manufacturers is spent on promotions, up from .5 percent in 1985.[1] This is one of the largest increases of **any expense item**. For many consumer packaged goods companies, promotions are the majority of their overall advertising expense.[2] Furthermore, the use of promotions is likely to increase in the future, as one of the limitations to performing more promotions is related to technology—something that vendors of promotion management software are alleviating by increasing the sophistication of their software. Sales and marketing, in fact, feel quite hamstrung by not being able to run more promotions. Some in sales and marketing question whether there may be too many promotions and whether they have negative consequences, but most of the sentiment lies with increasing the use of promotions.

---

[1] Hagemeyer,Dale. *Vendor Panorama for Trade Promotion Management in Consumer Goods.* Gartner, 2012.

[2] Lucas, Anthony. "In-Store Trade Promotions – Profit or Loss?" *Journal of Consumer Marketing.* April 1, 1996.

After reading a good deal of literature on promotions while researching for this book, what came across quite clearly is that authors in the field view promotions in a quite limited way. They point to the benefits to the company in terms of enhanced sales, but don't seem to appreciate that promotions have a cost. In fact, when costs are mentioned, they tend to be on the customer side—that is, the costs of brand erosion or the dangers of habituating customers to purchasing only during promotions. But the internal costs of promotions are rarely mentioned; those who work in sales and marketing look upon promotions as being **free** for the company to run. This is one of the major reasons as to why there are so many promotions currently, and why promotions are predicted to increase. This shunning of the internal cost question is apparent in two ways.

1. *Front-end Costs Are Minimized*: Those who focus on promotions rarely discuss the front-end costs of running the promotions, such as the costs of performing the market research to determine what the promotion should be, the cost of putting price changes through the system, the costs of hiring individuals to give out samples, or the costs of printing and distributing flyers and so on. However, almost completely absent from the writing on promotions are the back-end costs.

2. *Back-end Costs Are Minimized*: The back-end costs are those activities that are the primary topic of this book, including the following:
   1. *The costs of accounting for previous promotions in the sales history*
   2. *The costs of adjusting the forecast for future promotions*
   3. *The costs for the time spent communicating between sales/marketing and supply chain planning*
   4. *The costs for the time spent building promotional adjustment calculators*: This is performed in order to know by what magnitude the forecast should be adjusted.
   5. *The costs of extra inventory*: As very few companies account for all of their promotions in their demand history, the existence of promotions means increased lumpiness or variability in a company's demand history, which translates into higher average inventory carrying levels, which translates into higher costs.

The vast majority of the literature seems to assume that whatever the promotion does to increase sales will be magically accounted for by operations. However, promotions mean serious **costs** for the supply chain; sales/marketing is not accountable for these costs, but promotions also have costs for sales/marketing itself. I could not find either of these costs discussed in the literature on promotions, something I found quite amazing. If these costs were properly accounted for, promotions would seem quite a bit less appealing. The following quotation illustrates this point:

> *"CPG companies often spend anywhere from 8 percent to 20 percent of revenue on promotions. Various studies suggest that anywhere from 25 to 70 percent of CPG suppliers' trade promotion spend (their expenditure) is ineffective. Some quick math suggests that for every billion dollars in revenue, at least $20 million to $50 million and likely significantly more is being poorly spent. That is a substantial amount of money that could be better applied to product innovation or other more significant drivers of growth and brand equity."*
> – Uncovering the Hidden Costs of Trade Promotions

Promotions are an added complexity to any business. There is what is referred to as a churn, caused by constant promotions, that introduces chaos into the management of products.

> *"We have found that trade promotions can play havoc with the sales forecasting process, creating promotion-driven seasonality in historical sales data when distributors increase their inventories in response to periodic price promotions from manufacturers rather than to anticipated increases in consumer demand."*
> – Sales Forecasting Management

> *"With so many hands stirring the proverbial promotional pot, it is not uncommon for one item to be supported by multiple campaigns, each one of which is led by different sources across the enterprise. When this happens, 'double dipping' can occur, whereby the customer inadvertently receives multiple promotions on the same item.*

> *"'With hundreds of promotions happening across thousands of items simultaneously, oftentimes more than one department is promoting*

*the same item,' said Bob Smith, product manager for Retalix Loyalty.
'This becomes a critical business problem for everyone involved,
because not only will the item have a lower margin, it can even sell at
a loss.'"*

*When multiple promotions have different start and end dates,
retails also struggle to ensure that all prices are applied in the
correct sequence at the POS systems. But lack of automation,
synchronization and analytics keeps managers hard-pressed to
monitor whether promotions actually overlap correctly and end on
the specific dates, while ensuring that the right retail prices are
applied as soon as the promotion expires."*
                        – Centralization: The New Promotion Paradigm

As I have stated, sales/marketing would like to have more promotions. One
of the reasons they cannot increase the number of promotions is that they
are limited in their ability to implement the promotion. For instance, Retalix
makes software that automates the planning and implementation of promotions. They sell a centralized promotion management system, or "CPM," for
those companies that want to better control their promotions. However, some
of their functionality would make accounting for promotions for forecasting
purposes and forecasting promotions even more difficult.

*"If there is one promotion for $1 off an item that retails for $2.99,
and a similar promotion that offers the same product at $1.50,
shoppers can access two offers,' Smith said. 'Unless there is a
benchmark that can override this practice, shoppers will be able to
purchase the product as a combination of both offers—in this case,
for 50 cents—which would translate to a loss for the retailer.'"*
                        – Centralization: The New Promotion Paradigm

In fact, software vendors ranging from JDA to IBM to Junction Solutions make
promotion management software, and this category of software is quite broadly implemented at CPG clients. All of these applications are singularly focused
on allowing companies to implement increased numbers of and increased complexity of promotions. However, these applications do nothing to update the

promotion information in the forecasting system. Of course, any system can have its data extracted and put into another system with an interface, but this is clearly not the focus of the marketing literature of these software vendors. These software vendors also do not bother to mention the fact that there is increased overhead in accounting for promotions in demand history. Obviously they are simply focused on selling their software into companies by offering them tantalizing options to run increasingly complex promotions. Once again, the line of reasoning is that promotions are "free." They are "all benefit and no cost." What is at least somewhat amusing is that JDA, which sells this promotion management software, also sells forecasting software. However, once again JDA's marketing literature on promotion management software makes **no mention** of the overhead and complexity that all of these complicated promotions create for forecasting generally. Therefore, just as with the corporate buyers of software that often work towards conflicting objectives, JDA as a software vendor does the same thing in its other software lines. It offers functionality to sales/marketing that optimizes their needs at the expense of forecasting, while offering a forecasting solution that then attempts to deal with the extra forecasting complexity driven by the promotions that the company can now run more of because they purchased JDA's promotion management software. As is discussed in Chapter 6, "Accounting for Previous Promotions in Sales History" and Chapter 7, "Adding Promotions into the Forecast," the approaches covered use a **single** promotion price adjustment. In the future, if applications like Retalix become even more common—and there are multiple promotions for an item at one time—recording the change to demand will become **even more difficult**.

The upshot of this is that while forecasting in most companies is struggling mightily to keep up with the **present** frequency and complexity of promotions, Sales and Marketing is being pitched functionality by software companies that will enable the creation of even more complex promotional efforts. What seems to supply chain/forecasting departments as already excessive promotions, is considered simply an unfortunate and temporary limitation by Sales and Marketing.

"The technology also features an intuitive interface, making it easy to use for all personnel, including the creative team in marketing who

often feel hindered by rigid and inflexible information systems. With
access to promotional details and the ability to make changes without
the help of IT, marketing executives aren't restricted in finding new
and creative promotional solutions."
– Centralization: The New Promotion Paradigm

The Evidence for the Benefit of Promotions

This is the part of the book where I will ask a question that most companies
don't ask: What is the evidence regarding promotions and sales and profitability? Considering the popularity of promotions, the evidence for them is quite
mixed, and non-sales and non-marketing executives often take it for granted
that the benefits of promotions are quite substantial. However, once one looks
at the actual research into promotions, the benefits seems far less clear than
assumed.

> *"So do price promotions pay off? To answer that question, we*
> *analyzed seven years of scanner data, covering 25 product categories*
> *and 75 brands, from the Chicago area's second-largest supermarket*
> *chain, Dominick's Finer Foods. Previous research showed that price*
> *promotions tend to have little long-term effect on sales volume. Our*
> *new research found that the same is true for revenues and margins:*
> *They quickly snap back to baseline. But in the short-to-medium term,*
> *promotions can have very strong positive and negative effects that can*
> *hit retailers and manufacturers in very different ways."*
> – Who Benefits from Price Promotions?

This research actually does what so few companies do: measure the financial
benefits of the promotion. Interestingly, the benefits often accrue to different
members of the supply chain. This research tracked the promotion on cheese
that amounted to a reduction of ten cents per ounce, and the researchers used
scanning data from Dominick's Finer Foods supermarket.

> *"During the one-week promotion, the cheese manufacturer enjoyed*
> *an immediate $95,000 revenue increase as customers bought more*
> *of its brand. But the retailer saw a $130,000 loss, because gains*
> *from increased sales of the promoted brand were more than offset*

by defections from regularly priced brands. During the dust-settling weeks, two through six, the manufacturer saw a negative impact on revenue as customers migrated back to their usual brands and toward competing brands that had launched their own promotions. Meanwhile, retailer revenue for the cheese category gradually moved toward baseline as the promotion effects tailed off. By week six, manufacturer and retailer revenues had returned to their pre-promotion levels and remained stable through week 26.

*"This sequence of events is common: **A promotion increases manufacturer revenue and depresses retailer revenue in the short term but has no persistent effect for either party**. However, different types of promotions can affect revenues and margins in other ways. Promotions of frequently promoted brands, for example, tend to have a positive short-term effect on both retailers' and manufacturers' revenues but a negative impact on retailers' profit margins. Thus, the interests of manufacturers and retailers may well be aligned for one financial metric, such as revenue, but not for another, such as profit."*

– Who Benefits from Price Promotions?

Repeatedly, companies believe promotions are important in supporting their sales, but upon closer inspection, discover this to be untrue.

"One manufacturer of consumer products spent more than $100 million each year on trade promotions on the belief that these promotions stimulated demand and took market share away from its three major competitors. In the process of analyzing the company's sales forecasting needs, we conducted a series of regression-based forecasts. There seemed to be no relationship between dollars spent on trade promotions and company sales, industry sales or market share."

– Sales Forecasting

The other issue with promotions is that they are time-consuming to implement, and have become so frequent that they have been observed to train consumers to wait for promotions to stockpile the promoted item. That is, the frequent promotion can simply be a mechanism for increasing demand variability with a low net increase in extra consumption. In these cases the company loses in two dimensions: the first was just mentioned—the increased variability in sales (leading to more inventory)—and the second is in the lost profit from selling the promoted product at the normal versus the promotion price.

> *"In many sectors, brands are perceived as being on constant promotion, which results in consumer confusion as to the real price of the brand. In many cases marketing departments end up spending far too much time on trade initiatives while neglecting more value-added roles such as product innovation and brand franchise development."*
> – In-Store Trade Promotions – Profit or Loss?

This observation is echoed in a number of research papers on promotions. Furthermore, there is the issue of distraction, as promotions have increasingly become a major focus of sales/marketing, in many **cases to the exclusion of other activities they could be performing**. Promotions change the terms of sale, but they don't do anything aside from that. For instance:

1. They do not improve the understanding of the product, or improve the product, or improve its availability or service level.[3] These other features that make up the value of the product are areas that Sales/Marketing could also focus on.

2. They do not market the product in a unique or original way, positioning the product so it can be priced at a premium.

3. They do not provide insight to what customers like about the product that can help improve the product.

---

[3] In fact, due to the negative impact of promotions on forecasting, they most often reduce service level.

The Lack of Quantification with Respect to Planning Promotions

The costs of promotions, whether those costs are front-end or back-end, typically are **not** quantified within companies. Often promotions are not even compared with other expenditures such as normal advertising, although there is evidence that they really should be. A survey of U.S. companies has shown that those companies that spent 60 percent of their total budget on promotions underperformed companies that spent most of their budget on advertising instead of promotions.[4] In fact, beyond the discussion of whether to use promotions or what percentage of the advertising budget to apply to promotions, the way promotions are configured at companies seems driven mostly by guesswork; more often than not, companies do not have solid reasons for why they run promotions the way they do.

> *"Moreover, the costs and performance of trade promotions are highly variable and volatile. For example, certain promotional mechanisms such as multi-buys can be nearly twice as costly as extra weight. Off-the-shelf in-store promotions (i.e., end of aisle) tend to generate over seven times the incremental sales of on-the-shelf promotions. Ernst & Young research suggests that over 70 percent of off-the-shelf promotions generate a small profit contribution, whereas over 80 percent of on-the-shelf promotions may be loss making. Overall taking an average across a wide range of industries, while trade promotions appear to generate 10-20 percent incremental sales, a high proportion are loss making."*
> — In-Store Trade Promotions – Profit or Loss?

Some products tend to be promoted highly by companies, and others are not promoted, but often there is **no explanation** as to why this is the company's strategy. This again highlights the great degree of guesswork that seems to go hand-in-hand with promotions.

---

[4] Lucas, Anthony. "In-Store Trade Promotions – Profit or Loss?" *Journal of Consumer Marketing*. April 1, 1996.

"..sales ratios of certain key accounts were as high as 8 percent whereas others were as low as 2 percent. It came as no surprise to discover that promotional contributions differed markedly by key account. Again, in many cases there appeared to be no clear rationale or strategy for these variations. In the case of key accounts, costs and contributions seemed to be mainly influenced by the skills (both technical and self promotional) of the individual key account managers."

– In-Store Trade Promotions – Profit or Loss?

Loosely translated, in situations with unexplainable variances in the promotional allocations to different accounts, the promotions may be driven by the account managers themselves, the more experienced or connected account managers being able to gain access to a higher percentage of the overall promotional budget. These account managers (sales people) are not attempting to maximize the sales of the overall company, but maximize their personal sales. Those that can gain a leg-up by grabbing more of the promotional budget for themselves will often do so to help meet their individual sales goals. This is evidence that many promotions that are run by companies are not run because they are the right promotion, but because a sales person wants it to be run to meet his or her individual goals. The best way to allow some sales people to access a disproportionate amount of the promotion budget is to have **no firm rules** in place, and no research into what items are promoted. This is exactly the case in the majority of Sales and Marketing departments with which I have interacted.[5] This is reinforced by the paper "In Store Trade Promotions – Profit or Loss?," which explains that *"manufacturers need a better understanding of how much promotions cost and how their budgets are being spent, companies need to monitor continuously promotions by brand, mechanism, positioning and accounting and companies should seek to develop a model to help predict likely ROI."*

However, the question of control over the promotions leads to the question of who actually sets promotion policy in a company. Investigation into this area

---

[5] It also happens to be consistent with the research findings in this area.

shows a far less united front among the involved parties than is often assumed to be the case from the outside looking in.

The Power Struggle Between Sales and Marketing Over Promotions

Given the previous example of promotions being rigged by sales reps to gain an advantage over other sales reps, it is no surprise that Sales and Marketing (often represented as one entity in the book as Sales/Marketing), in fact frequently find themselves in heated debates over who will control promotions. Sales and Marketing have different incentives with respect to promotions, as Sales tends to take a more parochial view of promotions, with the alpha sales reps pulling the promotions budget away from other sales reps. Marketing has its own set of objectives that may not have a lot to do with the interests of the rest of the company. For instance, Marketing is under pressure to show benefits from their efforts in developing new products. A tremendous number of new products are introduced every year (most being really just slight variations of old products) and around 95 percent of new product introductions fail.[6] Marketing wants to promote new products to help these products succeed—and to validate their efforts in developing new products—but Sales is generally not going to care which products sell as long as the sales reps reach their quotas. This is one example of where the agendas of the two main controlling entities with respect to promotions diverge in their interests, but there are many other examples. With two sets of hands with conflicting objectives on the promotions steering wheel, it should come as no surprise that promotions strategies at most companies seem fractured.

Comparing Promotions Versus the "Everyday Low Price" Strategy

Sales/Marketing proposes that promotions will increase sales, and will do so in a way that will cover all costs for these promotions, but is never called upon to

---

[6]   Most new products that do succeed, do so by cannibalizing the sales of older products. No matter how many new varieties of toothpaste are brought out, it will not cause consumers to buy more toothpaste in aggregate. Therefore, the sales for new toothpaste varieties must come from the sales of current toothpaste varieties.

provide evidence that this is true. Furthermore, if we think about it logically, if temporary price reductions are a good thing, then what does that say about the company's standard price strategy? Is it set too high? For instance, if lower prices are better for a portion of the year, why not simply lower the prices (but by a lesser amount) for the entire year? Which one of these two strategies provides the highest profitability?

When I ask these questions in companies, I receive the types of answers that indicate that many promotions are created on the basis of feel, and that there are few analytics to support the promotions. This is supported by the research in this area as has already been referenced.

The following spreadsheet provides an answer to the question of whether a company should employ a variable price strategy (using promotions) or an "everyday low price" strategy for a particular SKU.

Promotion Versus Non Promotion Strategy

Product		Jan		Feb		Mar		Apr	Total Direct Profit
				Per Can					
Tunafish (variable price)	$	1.50	$	1.50	$	1.25	$	1.50	$ 34,750
Sales		20,000		18,000		24,000		19,500	
Tunafish (stable price)	$	1.35	$	1.35	$	1.35	$	1.35	$ 28,963
Sales		22,000		19,000		21,000		20,750	

Total External Cost of the Promotion	$	4,440	Cost / Can	$	1.00
Total Promotion Gain if Only Direct Profits are Considered	$	5,787			
Total Net Gain From Using Promotion Pricing	$	1,347			

This is the type of analysis that companies should be performing with respect to their promotions. If a product is to be placed on promotion, how a variable price strategy compares against an "everyday low price" strategy should already be assessed. In the example above, the price at which the product is sold has the cost of product subtracted, and then multiplied by the number of units sold at each price. When the costs of *running the promotion **are not** counted, the gains from the promotion seem large, at $5,787. However, if the costs are included, the profits drop very significantly to $1,347. (This is a made-up scenario designed to explain the framework for the analysis.)*

Why Sales/Marketing Want to Account for the Costs of Promotions

Without a full accounting of the costs of running promotions, it makes what Sales/Marketing does appear **more valuable** than it actually is; therefore, they prefer to not have a full accounting performed. And the example above did not even include the full costs of running the promotion because it did not include the costs of **reduced sales** to other products—that is, products that are cannibalized by the promotion. Frequently Sales/Marketing will bring up the point of increased profit from the sale of promoted SKUs, but not the profit loss of cannibalized products.

Promotion Profit Calculator

Product Category	Product	Percent Price Decrease	Relationship	Intial Forecast in Cases	Quantity Increase Due to Promotion	Profit Per Unit Sold	Profit Per Unit Sold
A	Tuna Fish	15%	(positive)8% Change in Volume Per 1% Change in Price	2,000	2,400	$ 0.25	$ 600.00
A	Swordfish	0%	(negative) 1.1% Change in Volume Per 1% Change in **Price of Tuna Fish**	3,200	(528.00)	$ 0.44	$ (232.32)
A	Mahi Mahi	0%	(negative) 2.7% Change in Volume Per 1% Change in **Price of Tuna Fish**	300	(121.50)	$ 0.35	$ (42.53)

Total Profit $ 325.16

This is another analysis that should be performed: how much is the gross profit of the promotion when accounting for cannibalized numbers? If only the profits for the promoted item are counted, the profits, before accounting for the costs of the promotion, appear to be $600. However, when all the profits from the reduced sales of cannibalized products are included, the benefits of the promotion look quite a bit different, with the company gaining only $325.16 in gross profits from the promotion.

The Incomplete Nature of Promotion Benefits Accounting

All of this demonstrates a major weakness of promotions: the gains from promotions **appear larger than they are** because only the enhanced sales are measured, or sometimes the profits that are generated from the promotion. However, without looking at the total costs, it is impossible to say if the promotion was worthwhile. Secondly, as long as some of the costs are external to the group that controls the promotion—which in fact is **always the case** with promotions, and adjusting forecast is just one example of the external cost—Sales/Marketing may have an incentive to continue to run marginal promotions, or indeed promotions that cause a net reduction in profit. It should be remembered that departments within companies operate towards their **own** incentives. One cannot rely upon individual departments to look out for the overall interests of the company. Rather, departments can be relied upon to engage in activities that maximize their own ability to meet their narrow objectives.

Conclusion

At many companies, promotions are a primary focus of Sales/Marketing and the use of promotions has grown very rapidly in addition to the proportion of company revenues that they consume. The literature from Marketing on promotions (which is the vast majority of literature that is written on the topic) seems to deliberately leave out many of the costs related to promotions. Many companies that run promotions do so reflexively because promotions are supposed to increase sales; however, because they generally don't pay attention to the research on promotions, they are not cognizant of how promotions are run. As a result, many companies are running mindless promotions that contribute little to profitability. While Sales/Marketing often views promotions as a universal virtue which brings universal benefits, the research on promotions indicates that the benefits are much more uncertain or variable. This also is true of vendors in the area of promotions management software. They give their customers even more ability to run promotions than they already have. A major reason for the discrepancy of how promotions are measured in academic studies and the optimism with respect to promotions in companies is a question of accounting. Sales/Marketing can run promotions that are a net loss for the company while enhancing their ability to meet sales goals. For Sales/Marketing the focus is sales, not profits.

Promotions come out of the budget for Sales and/or Marketing, and therefore promotions are primarily controlled by Sales or Marketing. Promotions are the primary way companies get customers of another brand to switch to their brand. In many companies, Sales and Marketing increasingly views promotions as a major part of the overall strategy. For many consumer packaged goods companies, promotions are the majority of their overall advertising expense. The vast majority of the literature seems to assume that whatever the promotion does to increase sales will be magically accounted for by operations. However, promotions mean serious costs for the supply chain; Sales/Marketing is not accountable for these costs, but promotions also have costs for Sales/Marketing itself. Non-sales and non-marketing executives often take it for granted that the benefits of promotions are quite substantial. However, once one looks at the actual research into promotions, the benefits seems far less clear than assumed. Sales/Marketing proposes that promotions will increase sales, and will do so in a way that will cover all costs for these promotions, but is never called upon to provide evidence that this is true. In the next chapter we will see how promotions impact the supply chain.

CHAPTER 3

Promotions from Supply Chain's Perspective

From the supply chain's perspective, promotions are entirely negative. Promotions cause distortions in the demand history when (and this is most often the case) the promotion is not accounted for—that is, when the sales from the promotion are not identified as promotions within the statistical forecasting system. However, supply chain departments are also resigned to the fact that they cannot control promotions.

Supply chain is responsible for providing the stock availability when promotions are scheduled. Promotions take time and effort to manage; however, the supply chain is simply required to manage promotions and does not receive more funding to effectively manage promotions. From the outside looking in, promotions may not seem to cost very much, but the more one investigates and the more time one spends in companies that do engage in promotions, the more the costs of promotions become apparent. According to Uncovering the Hidden Costs of Trade Promotions, some of these costs include:

1. *"Wasted material*

2. *Excess inventory*

3. *Reduced customer service levels*

4. *Out of stocks (and lost sales)*

5. *Labor to break down unused displays*

6. *Transportation to ship product between DCs*

7. *Inefficient sourcing of raw materials such as corrugate, components, chemicals*

8. *Re-pricing at the retail location (both prior to and after the promotion)*

9. *Inefficient sourcing of co-packing vendor capacity*

10. *Upcharges for 'rush' orders*

11. *Lack of utilization of "'postponement'*

12. *Upstream planning problems result in reactive and inefficient downstream production and distribution (e.g., delaying creation of display to as late as possible)"*

People tend to underemphasize that promotions create a large amount of chaos in the supply chain. Promotions cause unnatural bulges or lumpiness in demand. These are not uncontrollable bulges in demand that are a natural consequence of consumer behavior; these are bulges in demand that are actually **initiated** by the company itself.

Many products that one would not think of as being lumpy are made lumpy by the direct actions of the company. This is the exact opposite of what any supply chain wants. This "unnecessary lumpiness" is caused primarily by the following:

1. Sales and Marketing offering promotions.

2. Sales and Marketing introducing new products without culling the database for products that have poor demand. The same amount of demand over more products will tend to translate into more variability and lower forecastability.

Supply chain, on the other hand, would prefer to smooth out the demand, as they must purchase the input product, produce the item, and push it through the supply network. This works more efficiently when the volume has the lowest possible variability. Promotions interfere with this, and therefore promotions will never be popular with those who focus on supply chain.

Bulges in demand are also inefficient because a supply chain—and in fact any infrastructure—works better when it works slightly under capacity, a fact that is not well understood because many believe that maximum efficiency **can be reached at capacity**. However, studies into manufacturing facilities shows that managers should not attempt to staff their factories for the expected capacity, but should slightly overstaff in order to gain maximum efficiency. This rule applies to any capacity, be it factory, a road system or a supply chain. Running at capacity is a dangerous situation because the slightest bump can cause one to exceed capacity, and the result of this is contention. The most common manifestation of this for us in our daily lives is the dreaded traffic jam.

A supply chain is a network of suppliers, plants, distribution centers, pallet spaces, trucks and the like that allow a company to meet demand. Any supply chain has a certain maximum throughput. This throughput can be enlarged, but at a cost, and most often at a loss of efficiency. For instance, at certain times of the year, many companies enhance their storage capacity with either offsite storage or by parking trailers filled with product outside of their distribution centers. Both of these storage costs are higher than when the native storage capacity is used. Beyond the incremental costs, there is a loss in efficiency, as product must be transported back and forth between the distribution centers and offsite storage. Having many containers in the yard of the distribution center can also lead to quality degradation, as the environment of a container or trailer may not be as conducive to the integrity of the product as storage in the distribution center itself. Using offsite storage also leads to extra time spent looking around for product, or moving trailers around to access the trailers with the desired material. When these types of actions are taken in order to meet, say, a seasonal demand, it is considered obligatory as some demand simply fluctuates around seasons or events. One would not want to incur the expense of building permanent capacity if the seasonal spike is significantly above the normal demand level. However, a promotion is different; it is optional, as a promotion is entirely at the discretion of the entity that is running the promotion.

CHAPTER 4

Common Issues with Promotional Forecasting

The most common issues with respect to promotional forecasting are the following:

1. Companies often do not account for promotions in their sales history.

2. Companies do not maintain a database through which they can extrapolate the future changes in demand in response to promotions.

3. Sales and Marketing often does not communicate to supply chain when future promotions will be held. Secondly, Sales and Marketing is not held responsible for communicating future promotions to supply chain.

Is Extra Complexity Simply Managed with Systems?

Most sales and marketing types, as well as many strategy consultants (none of whom are normally supply chain experts, by the way), propose that extra complexity added by sales and marketing should not be a problem, and that supply chain should simply adapt to more product proliferation and all other complexities introduced by

Sales and Marketing. Advanced planning software and optimizers, and advanced forecasting algorithms can manage these issues. (Either that, or they propose that "Lean" can do it; whatever the complexity, there is—according to them—a special magic box that can make an inefficient business model design all better.) Of course, if you don't have to personally do something, all kinds of possibilities open up in terms of ways to make improvements. Interestingly, and completely unknown to most strategy consultants, the less forecastable a product, the less useful (**not more useful**) advanced methods become. Extremely lumpy products may as well be placed on reorder point planning. Reorder point planning requires no forecast and creates orders on the basis of falling below an inventory level, which is how planning was performed before MRP was introduced. The less erratic the sales history, the more forecastable the PLC and the more a forecasting system can do with the history—the exact opposite of those who propose that complex solutions can solve the problems of poor planning.

Product Proliferation

Product proliferation is the increase in the number of products that are carried. Often the marketing differences between the products are only incidental and illusory. Proliferation would be even worse than it currently is, but retailers only have so much space to offer. An excellent example of product proliferation is toothpaste.

*Most of these toothpaste containers contain essentially a similar set of chemical com-
pounds; however, marketing provides customers with different varieties of what is often the same product in order to promote purchases. Many of the claims are unfounded,
but because there is very little regulation (in the U.S. at least), one can say what they
like regarding what the toothpaste will do for consumers. Whether something is true
or not is barely mentioned (that is what is written on the packaging), and anyone who
might bring this up is considered hopelessly naïve as the primary focus is whether or
not the claim will increase sales.*

> *"Retailers are faced by increasing assortment. In grocery retail,
> product life cycles have been decreasing. As a consequence it is
> increasingly difficult to forecast sales for an individual item in a
> particular store for tactical reasons, as time series tend to be short.
> Moreover retail sales are faced with extensive promotion activities.
> Products are typically on promotion for a limited period of time, e.g.
> one week during which demand is usually substantially higher than
> during periods without promotion, and many stock outs occur during
> promotions due to inaccurate forecasts."*
> – SKU Demand Forecasting in the Presence of Promotions

There may be no better example of an industry that has gone to the extreme
with unnecessary product proliferation as the grocery industry. The typical
U.S. grocery store has between 35,000 and 50,000 SKUs, which is a massive
increase in SKUs over the past several decades. When standing, one can no
longer see over most grocery store shelves. However, one grocery chain takes a
different path, and this is a major reason they perform so much better than the
industry average. I covered Trader Joe's in my first forecasting book, *Supply
Chain Forecasting Software*.

Trader Joe's has put its supply chain in a better position than almost every
other grocery store in the U.S. Trader Joe's carries fewer SKUs. Having fewer
lower-turning SKUs as a percentage of the database means that Trader Joe's
is in a better position to have a **lower forecast error**, and therefore a more
efficient management of their inventory than would a typical supermarket.

This means doing what is an anathema to Sales/Marketing: actually **discontinuing** products. Trader Joe's policy regarding discontinuing products is
available right on the FAQ page of their website.

"Question: Why does TJ's frequently discontinue products?
Answer: Our mission is to bring you the best quality products at the best
prices. To do this, we have to manage our store space well. Each of our prod-
ucts must 'stand on its own,' meaning it must pay its own way. Each prod-
uct passes certain criteria in order to earn its way onto our shelves – includ-
ing a rigorous tasting panel.
There may be several factors that determine why we discontinue products:

1. *It may be a seasonal product - for example, strawberries, which are in*
   season only specific times of the year.

2. *The gang-way factor - because we introduce 10-15 new products a week,*
   we have to eliminate 10-15 items in order to give our newest items a fair
   chance.

3. *The cost of producing the item may increase, which would in turn in-*
   crease the cost to you - if the item is not a strong seller, we may choose to
   discontinue it."

This strategy, which is so good for the supply chain, is also good for profitability:

> *"Trader Joe's primary success factor has been its inventory sourcing*
> *and pricing model. Specifically, Trader Joe's limits its stock to*
> *specialty products that it can sell at very low prices. This is done by*
> *purchasing large quantities of specialty goods (that do not interest*
> *conventional supermarkets) and thereby securing low prices. This*
> *allows customers to purchase unique products while guaranteeing*
> *value."*
> > – Trader Joe's vs. Whole Foods Market: A Comparison of
> > Operational Management

Trader Joe's is a contrarian in many respects, and they also **do not engage** in promotions.

> *"Simplicity helps. By shunning major brands and broad product*
> *offerings, Trader Joe's avoids the complex supply-chain and*
> *marketing issues that dog most rivals. Instead, it targets a brie-*

and-chardonnay audience with private-label brands and almost no
promotion, stocking only items it can sell at a bargain price and still
turn a profit."

– The Grocery Chain That Should Not Be

An interesting question one might ask is, if promotions are so important in driving sales, why is Trader Joe's so successful without using them? Trader Joe's is the type of company that Sales and Marketing would like to go away, because it leads to all the "wrong" type of conclusions. How successful is Trader Joe's? Trader Joe's falls into a category of companies that is so successful, its natural constraints in growth can actually lead to a backlash against its brand, as the following quotation explains.

"However most of the early reviews didn't discuss the great food but
rather how tough it was to park one's car. Traffic on the highway
snarled and excited customers resorted to parking in the lots of
neighboring merchants— who had no problem calling tow trucks.
One victim was a retired judge. Things got snarky, and local media
covered the parking pitfalls with great verve. What's interesting to me
is that Trader Joe's is actually the victim of a very rare occurrence
in marketing known as 'catastrophic success.' High demand coupled
with limited supply and poor delivery lead to backlash, which can
actually damage a brand. It almost never happens."

– The Grocery Chain That Should Not Be

This type of thing does not happen to Safeway, Kroger, or any of the other traditional supermarkets, all of which engage in heavy and constant promotions. Generally people don't write letters to Safeway or Kroger begging them to open a store in their neighborhood, but this does happen to Trader Joe's. Beyond promotions, Trader Joe's also does not engage in other common marketing activity—notably a loyalty program, which is quite common in almost every other grocery store. This is explained on the Trader Joe's website.

"'Sale' is a four-letter word to us. We have low prices, every day. No
coupons, no membership cards, no discounts. You won't find any
glitzy promotions or couponing wars at our stores. If it makes you feel

any better, think of it as all our items are on sale, day in and day out."

However, they do offer samples, which is a type of promotion. And they seem to do this year-round. Almost always, something is offered at the counter in the back of the store, although it seems rather low in scale. For instance, I might try a sample every third or fourth visit.

Going Against the Grain

Trader Joe's does something amazing in this day and age: they actually give supply chain and operations a place at the table, and allow them to co-develop the strategy and policies with Sales and Marketing. How is this possible? Sales and Marketing (primarily at the food companies, which control the theme and orientation of supermarkets) have turned most U.S. supermarkets into plastic environments, packed to the gills with massive product proliferation which has high costs of forecasting and high supply chain costs. Recovering these costs means offering more varieties of processed foods, which have higher margins and which can sit longer due to their high concentrations of preservatives. In fact, if your inventory turns are **slow** because you have proliferated your product database, you simply cannot afford to keep a large percentage of fresh food. Trader Joe's, on the other hand, by designing a simpler model, finds itself in a positive feedback loop. It can keep its prices low (even for a better product) because its supply chain efficiency is so much higher than the industry average. Trader Joe's can offer a freshness level in its food that the major supermarkets simply can't match. Those who ignore the rules of supply chain pay a price in one shape or form. Most companies make things as difficult for themselves as possible, and then complain about poor operational performance. However, operational performance is bound by the strategy that is set forth through the interaction of the different interest groups within the company. Supply chain knows that promotions are another area that essentially helps to make its life difficult. Even with this extra complexity, supply chain groups within companies do not do nearly enough to manage the promotional effect.

Conclusion

Now that we have completed all of the background information regarding promotions, it's almost time to address how to manage promotions for effective forecasting. However, in order to understand this topic, it is important to consider a foundational topic that is referred to as forecastability. Promotions decrease the forecastability of a PLC and the lower the forecastability, the more likely it is that a level forecast will be created, and the more likely it is that more inventory will have to be carried. Therefore, forecastability is the topic of the next chapter.

Trader Joe's has a level of customer service that almost every other supermarket in the U.S. could only dream of attaining. They do not engage in promotions; yet, most of the industry copies the standard supermarket model of offering promotions. Very little in the way of evidence actually directs business strategy; interest groups within companies, looking out for their parochial concerns, are far more important in decisions around strategy.

CHAPTER 5

Forecastable Versus Unforecastable Products

I have analyzed a good deal of product databases over the years, and many of the products that I have analyzed from different companies are clearly unforecastable. There is a simple reason for this. Many products that are difficult to forecast have no discernible pattern in their demand history, and without a discernible pattern, no mathematical algorithm can create a good forecast. This is not generally understood. Part of the reason that too much effort is spent on very hard-to-forecast products is due to a misimpression about when statistical forecasting can add value, and when it can't. This is well said by Michael Gilliland in *The Lean Approach to Forecasting*:

> *The best a forecaster ever can do is discover the underlying structure or rule guiding the behavior that is being forecast, finding a model that accurately represents the underlying behavior—and then hoping that the underlying behavior doesn't change. Unfortunately, there is an element of randomness that surrounds virtually all behavior, and the degree of randomness will limit the accuracy you can achieve.*

One of the first questions to ask is whether there is value to actively generating a forecast. In some cases the answer is no. However, instead of recognizing that a product is not forecastable and adjusting to this reality, more sophisticated mathematics are often employed in a vain attempt to improve the forecast. Clients I have worked for in the past have adopted this philosophy, as have the majority of consultants and vendors I have worked with, and this philosophy is also reflected in forecasting academic papers I have read. Since so many well-educated people agree on this thinking, it must be correct—right? Well actually they don't all agree. A number of academics have written on the concept of unforecastable products, but for some reason their research does not seem to get sampled and disseminated. However, the scholarly literature is not objectively sampled. In fact, most forecasting consultants in don't read it at all. Proven approaches like turning off forecasating for unforecastable products leads to short, and insufficiently lucrative consulting engagements. Deloitte, Accenture, IBM, etc.. are not going to implement any proven and low cost forecasting approach, when a far more expensive but ineffective approach is available to them.

However, there is little evidence that sophisticated mathematics can improve the forecast of difficult-to-forecast products, and this is a problem. Some studies do not show improvement from more advanced methods. But first, the improvement is never very large, and secondly other studies come by later to contradict the original studies. In addition, complex methods should have to exceed a higher bar. Academics can apply complex methods in a laboratory environment over a few products far more easily than can be done by industry. This fact, along with the point that sophisticated methods are much more expensive for industry to implement than simple methods, is rarely mentioned. This point is made very well by J. Scott Armstrong:

> *Use simple methods unless a strong case can be made for complexity.*
> *One of the most enduring and useful conclusions from research*
> *on forecasting is that simple methods are generally as accurate*
> *as complex methods. Evidence relevant to the issue of simplicity*
> *comes from studies of judgment (Armstrong 1985), extrapolation*
> *(Armstrong 1984, Makridakis et al. 1982, and Schnaars 1984), and*
> *econometric methods (Allen and Fildes 2001). Simplicity also aids*
> *decision makers' understanding and implementation, reduces the*
> *likelihood of mistakes, and is less expensive.*

The Inconvenient Truth About Statistical Forecasting

For statistical forecasting, the only products that can be forecasted are those that have a discernible pattern to their demand history, and not all products have this pattern. Forecastability can usually be determined—or at least indicated—without any math by simply observing a line graph of a product's three-year demand history. If there is no discernible pattern, it is unlikely that the product is forecastable with mathematical methods. (Products that are using just the last few periods to create a forecast are the exception to this rule.) An algorithm that can appear to be predictive can be built for unforecastable products, but more often than not this is an illusion created by the forecaster who over-fitted the forecast. As is pointed out by Michael Gilliland, just because a model can be built to match the past, does not mean it should be used to perform forecasting:

> *The statistical approach is based on the assumption that there is a structure or pattern in the behavior we are trying to forecast. As human beings, we are very good at finding structure and pattern in the world around us—even when none exists. Clouds look like poodles, a burnt cheese sandwich reveals the Virgin Mary, and an ant's innocent meandering in the sand caricatures Winston Churchill. We readily come up with lucid explanations of the ups and downs of the stock market and of demand for our products and services. Unfortunately, the patterns we see may not be real, and even if they are, we have no assurance they will continue into the future.*

Products that have a very stable history exist at the other end of the continuum of forecast difficulty. Typically, it is very easy to forecast for products with a stable demand history; however, if this is the case, actively forecasting the product does not add very much value to supply planning (the ultimate consumer of the demand plan) because a product with stable demand history does not *need* to be forecasted. Products with stable demand can be managed effectively and efficiently with reorder point logic, where orders are based upon a reorder point or a reorder period.

Very stable and very unstable products converge in their forecasting approach, as is evidenced by the fact that a many-period moving average is equally useful for products with both a stable demand history and products with an unstable demand history. When both stable and unstable demand history products are run through a best-fit forecasting procedure, the normal result is that both will be fitted with a stable or level forecast. Companies have a very strong tendency to actively forecast all items in their product database without first asking the following question:

> *What is the value added by forecasting for the different product categories?*

However, the rule of thumb is simple:

> *A forecast adds value to the supply planning process when the demand planning system is creating a forecast for a product for which there is a discernible pattern for demand and if the forecast is not simply a constant or relatively constant value.*

Creating forecasts for the entire product database for S&OP forecasting or for other purposes may be important and necessary. However, the forecasting process that results in a demand plan being sent to supply planning can be segregated based on the rule of the value added to supply planning.

Intermittent or Lumpy Demand

Intermittent—or "lumpy"—demand is one of the most common features of a product's demand history that makes a product unforecastable. Service parts are the best-known example of a product with lumpy demand. However, I have come across intermittent demand in many different types of companies. For instance, one of my clients was a textbooks publisher. A large percentage of their product database had an intermittent demand history which would normally not be expected of this type of product. However, due to the fact that different US states buy textbooks in large volumes whenever funding comes through, the demand ends up being quite unpredictable for many books. A school system will not make any purchase for some time, and then will buy many textbooks all at once. For example, California is on a seven-year procurement cycle, which means they wait seven years between purchases.

And this is a very important distinction that explains why demand, which one would expect to be forecastable, is much less forecastable in reality. This is because many products have significant lags and batching between procurement and consumption, unrelated to EOQ-driven ordering. In the case of this textbook publisher, the intermittency was related to when state funding was approved for textbook purchases.

"Demand shaping" is the term used to describe how companies influence purchasing behavior so that demand is less intermittent and more predictable (typically through offering incentives). Demand shaping is a popular concept and is a very good idea in principle. Unfortunately, a term has not been coined to describe the opposite of demand shaping (demand wrecking?), but it is common practice among the majority of companies. Most companies actively increase the intermittency of demand (thus reducing the product's forecastability) by doing things like creating promotions and instituting end-of-quarter sales "pushes." Customers respond to these behaviors by further batching their demand. It is well known that eventually customers become habituated to end-of-quarter price reductions and postpone their buying in anticipation of the end of the quarter. There are a host of other programs often initiated by companies that make demand less forecastable than it ordinarily would be if natural or true demand were received. Michael Gilliland reinforces exactly what I have seen inside of companies.

> *Many organizational practices (such as promotional activities,*
> *sales contests, and quarter-end push) only serve to increase volatility.*
> *Typical practices are designed to produce record sales weeks rather*
> *than promote smooth, consistent and profitable growth…Rather than*
> *creating costly incentives to spike demand, it may make more sense to*
> *design incentives that smooth demand.*

> *Management has control over the often-misguided policies and practices*
> *that serve to increase volatility, and management can change them*
> *One of the surest and cheapest ways to get better forecasts is to simply*
> *make the demand forecastable.*

It's important to understand how much demand shaping would change the business landscape. Demand shaping would mean removing the policies that increase intermittency and offering incentives to smooth demand beyond the customer's natural purchasing frequency, to better match the company's supply capability. This is a tall order, and it must be understood that normally demand planning cannot do anything about the company's sales incentive policies as these are controlled by the Sales or Marketing departments. These departments have historically been insensitive to problems they impose upon operations. Secondly, in the US at least, Sales and Marketing have been much more powerful than operations for decades. This point is brought up in the book, *Factory Physics*:

> *The influences of the golden era on the current condition of American manufacturing are subtle and complex. Besides promoting a de-emphasis on manufacturing details, the emphasis on marketing and finance in the 1950s and 1960s profoundly influenced today's American manufacturing firms. Recognizing these areas as having the greatest career potential, more and more of the "best and brightest" chose careers in marketing and finance. These became the glamour functions, while manufacturing and operations were increasingly viewed as "career breakers."*

The erosion of operations' influence has steadily continued, with sales, marketing and finance setting policy, and operations being forced to execute this policy with very little in the way of input. Management books talk about how the world should be, with a company's departments coming together to make joint decisions that are highly rational and integrative. However, the reality is that the politically powerful departments get their way regardless of how the policy affects other departments. Sales, marketing and finance see themselves as the departments within the company that add value, while operations is essentially viewed as commodity.

Many companies have already made outsourcing the manufacturing function. If it could be done feasibly, companies would like to outsource all nonmanufacturing supply chain functions as well! However, outsourcing other supply chain functions is not really feasible, as third party logistics never came close to its promise of integrating these capabilities. This topic is covered on the SCM Focus sub-site "fourth party logistics":

http://www.scmfocus.com/fourthpartylogistics/

This is why it is hard to see demand shaping as having much of a future. Any real enthusiasm on this topic would come at the expense of incentives and recognizing how they are structured within companies. Moving to demand shaping would mean sales and marketing completely changing the way they do business to be in line with the long term interests of the company. It would also mean giving up the power they currently enjoy to destroy value. This is clear also from the airline industry. In the US for decades now one airline has lead all others in on-time performance, customer service and profitability.[1] This is an operationally driven company which invests little in marketing. This airline is called Southwest, and although they could easily be copied, none of the major airlines do so, preferring their old sales and marketing and customer dissatisfaction approach. Why? I would argue that while all the major airlines could improve all of their performance metrics by moving to the Southwest model, they haven't because sales and marketing would have their power eroded. And because the airline business is monopolistic, they can afford to continue to operate in this fashion.

ToolsGroup and Lumpy Demand

Of the vendors I have analyzed, probably the one (that does not specialize in service parts) with the greatest focus on demand intermittency is ToolsGroup. This is consistent with ToolsGroup's orientation toward planning, as is demonstrated in the screen shot below:

---

[1] Although SouthWest has more recently seen its performance in some categories decline.

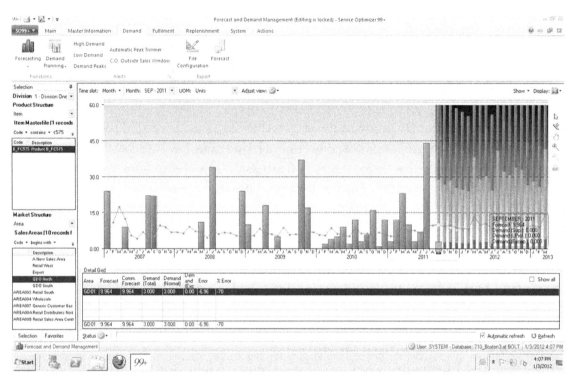

Notice that with ToolsGroup, the lumpiness shows in the demand history. However, the future lines on the dark background are very long. This is called the prediction interval, which is the range over which a forecast is likely to fall. On a lumpy product like this one, notice how large the range is when compared to the more predictable demand pattern below:

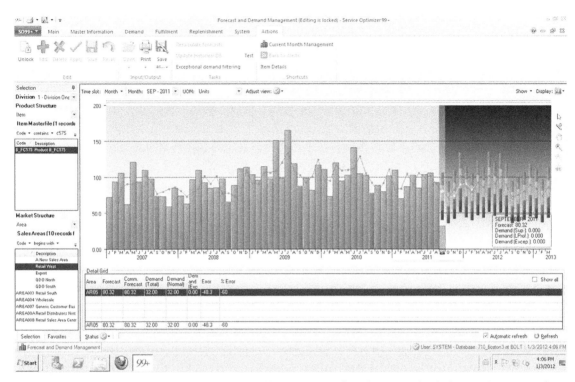

The more predictable item has a smaller range of values. It is inherently more forecastable. ToolsGroup's interface allows to me to demonstrate a basic concept about forecasting, which is what a good user interface should be able to do.

Trends in Lumpiness Case Study 1: Trader Joe's Versus Normal Supermarkets

Across different industries, lumpy or erratic demand histories are becoming more common. ToolsGroup has also observed this phenomenon and wrote about it in their white paper, "Mastering Lumpy Demand". One reason for the increased prevalence of lumpy demand histories is that the number of products that must be planned keeps increasing. This would not be a problem if the growth in the number of products matched the growth in demand, but it doesn't; the number of products easily outpaces the growth in demand. This is referred to as product proliferation, and is driven by the introduction of new products without the removal of low volume items from the product database. Product proliferation is described in many articles and research papers, although strangely the phenomenon is not usually tied back to forecasting. Product proliferation reduces forecastability, meaning, of course, that the company must carry more inventories. The increased costs imposed on the supply chain because of product proliferation are generally not estimated.

The increased number of SKUs maintained by companies can be used to quantify product proliferation. Simply comparing pictures of older grocery stores to present day supermarkets can also make it obvious. Today's supermarkets are so much larger and so filled with variety, they would be unrecognizable to people from previous eras. According to the Food Marketing Institute, present-day supermarkets carry between 15,000 and 60,000 SKUs, with the average being around 45,000.[2]

Trader Joe's, still in operation today, is representative of grocery stores that maintained fewer SKUs in the past. Trader Joe's is a specialty food retailer (they can't really be called a supermarket) and they carry approximately 4,000 SKUs per store. Unlike supermarkets that have a high number of low-turning SKUs, Trader Joe's eliminates poor selling items. This strategy allows them to have a sales per square foot figure that is twice that of Whole Foods, another very successful grocery chain, and places them in a much better position from a forecasting and overall supply chain planning perspective. With fewer SKUs and fewer lower-turning SKUs as a percentage of the database, Trader Joe's is in a better position to have a lower forecast error, and therefore, more efficient management of their inventory than would a typical supermarket. This also translates into a lower cost supply chain. Many strategy consultants and software salesmen like to tell their clients that any complexity added to the supply chain can be managed with advanced tools and advanced techniques. This is incorrect, and most of the people making these claims do not know enough about supply chain management or software to make these proposals. Part of a supply chain's efficiency and resulting costs is a function of the discipline that is employed to limit the number of products. One step in this direction is to reduce product proliferation. However, Trader Joe's rational approach to SKU management is an anomaly; the fact is, product proliferation is here to stay.

---

[2] Something that is not frequently discussed is that this proliferation is only possible because products are now shipped from such vast distances, meaning grocery items can be produced in one location and shipped thousands of miles away. The average produce in a supermarket travels 1,500 miles between the farm and the retail location.

Trends in Lumpiness Case Study 2: Netflix and the Long Tail

A second example of increasing lumpy demand history is found in the movement toward online retailing. The Internet has provided some companies[3] with the ability to sell online, satisfy demand from fewer distribution points, and still hold and offer a much wider number of SKUs. Companies like Netflix leverage online storefronts and national distribution networks to offer more selection than ever before. To immediately grasp this development, consider the demand history of a single Blockbuster Video store (back when Blockbuster dominated the video rental space) versus the present day Netflix distribution point. Netflix carries roughly 100,000 unique titles and ships out roughly 35,000 titles, or a third of its title variety, every day. Netflix is differentiated in the video rental market by its selection of titles—the broadest available. All of Netflix's national demand is distributed over fifty-eight distribution points (as of 2011). At its height in 2009, Blockbuster Video had 4,500 stores in the US and carried roughly 6,500 unique titles per store.[4]

Netflix currently operates roughly (58/6,500) or 1/112th as many distribution points as Blockbuster Video did at its zenith, and carries roughly (100,000/4,500) twenty-two times as many unique titles. This means that even with twenty-two times the number of unique titles, Netflix is in a position to manage its inventory more efficiently than a Blockbuster Video store. A Blockbuster Video store could hold only a fraction of the titles that Netflix can, and therefore, could only carry high-demand items. In the video market, title selection is a very important factor in customer satisfaction, and Netflix's intelligently designed network of warehouses provides this selection. Therefore, Netflix's added value over Blockbuster Video, even when Netflix was just starting out, was tremendous, and their distribution network gave them such a price advantage and greater convenience, that once

---

[3] Not all products are a good fit for being sold online as the online grocery store WebVan learned.

[4] Actually, one way that Blockbuster Video became so popular was by offering more titles and better inventory management capabilities over many smaller, independently operated stores. However, even with that number of titles, Blockbuster Video stores concentrated their inventory in recently released titles. Blockbuster Video was the leader in DVD inventory management, but no physical store-based inventory model can compete with what is essentially a direct-from-warehouse inventory model.

Netflix became widely known, the store-based rental market, including Blockbuster Video, went into rapid decline. Blockbuster Video had an enormous head start, much better brand recognition, greater financial resources, etc., than did Netflix.

However, Netflix had the better design. Netflix is known as an Internet phenomenon and while their website is, in fact, excellent, they are equally a supply chain management phenomenon.

Netflix carries roughly 93,500 more titles than each Blockbuster Video store did.[5] Clearly, with so many titles, some of which are "specialty" titles, Netflix happens to have more lumpy demand for their less popular items. Netflix is one example of a company that is exploiting hyper selection to attract and retain customers, and Amazon.com is another. The fact is that Internet storefronts allow companies to carry more items than they ever could in physical storefronts. However, this also means increased numbers of lower or lumpy demand products in the mix which must be managed by demand planning systems.

Now that we have described some of the factors driving the increase in lumpy demand history, we will describe one of the major myths related to dealing with difficult-to-forecast products.

Dealing with Lumpy Demand with Complex Methods

Lumpy or intermittent demand is the bane of effective forecasting. One of the major approaches to dealing with difficult-to-forecast products has been to apply increasingly sophisticated forecasting methods, the results of which have generally not been positive. However, this has not changed the belief that using more complex forecasting methods is an effective strategy. Executives often see complex forecasting methods as a magic bullet. In fact, it seems that the more indecipherable the forecasting method, the higher its status, as exemplified by one of the major intermittent forecasting methods called Croston's. Croston's has been a source of hope for executive decision makers to improve the forecasting of lumpy demand

---

[5] An exact approximation is not possible as some stores carried different titles, so the number of total unique titles in the system was higher. However, every title was not available at every Blockbuster Video store, whereas every Netflix title is available to every Netflix customer.

items since it was first incorporated in enterprise demand planning software. It's difficult to see where all of this confidence and enthusiasm is coming from, as various research papers on Croston's are inconclusive regarding its benefits.

Wayne Fu, at Servigistics[6] and myself analyzed Croston's and determined that it would only improve the forecast over much more simple methods in a very small number of situations. This article is available at the link below:

   http://www.scmfocus.com/demandplanning/2010/07/crostons-vs-smooth-ie-methods/

Therefore, forecast methods that are too complex to be easily understood, backward engineered and placed into Excel, are not particularly beneficial as they are frequently emulated by simpler methods. In fact, the forecasting methods that are actually being used at most companies tend to be quite simple, and the obsession with the complex methods is mostly smoke. Complex methods seem to hold the continual promise of improved forecast accuracy, but are much less frequently implemented than simple methods.

Croston's is one of the most complex forecasting algorithms used in demand planning, and few people understand the exact mathematics for what it does. This is, in my view, why it continues to be popular regardless of its value in improving forecast accuracy. In fact, it's not difficult to predict that Croston's will continue to be popular because of the general and entirely unfounded belief that difficult-to-forecast products benefit from more sophisticated mathematical forecasting models. Commercial incentives and pressures are at play in both what vendors offer in their applications and what is written about forecasting. New forecast methodologies are not necessarily developed because they are superior to simpler and easier-to-implement techniques, but because they help get research papers published and help sell software and obtain consulting contracts. Some complex forecasting methods are incorporated into applications simply because clients demand them. One software vendor I am familiar with added Croston's to their product, not because they thought it was going to be beneficial to custom-

---

[6] A service parts planning vendor. Because they work in the service space, they are of course, very experienced with forecasting lumpy demand history.

ers, but because executives kept asking for it. Adding Croston's made their applications seem more "leading edge." The lack of benefit from more complex methods is described in J. Scott Armstrong's research paper "Conclusions of 25 Years of Research", quotes from which I have listed below:

> *More important, Table 1 provides little evidence to suggest that sophistication beyond the methods available in the 1960s has had any payoff. Relatively simple methods seem to offer comparable accuracy; twenty-one studies concluded that there were negligible differences, and for the eighteen studies showing differences, eleven favored sophistication, and seven favored simplicity. However, of the eleven cases favoring sophistication, three have since been challenged, and three cases were based on the superiority of exponential smoothing (available prior to 1960). We are left with five comparisons favoring sophistication and seven favoring simplicity.*

> *In general, the findings on sophisticated methods are puzzling, and it is unlikely that they could have been anticipated in 1960. Many of the sophisticated methods made good sense. For example, it seemed reasonable to expect that models in which the parameters are automatically revised as new information comes in should be more accurate.*

However, more complex methods can produce the illusion of producing a more accurate forecast because they often fit better with demand history. This is called "over-fitting" and was pointed out by Michael Gilliland earlier in this chapter.

> *Highly complex models may reduce accuracy. While these complex models provide better fits to historical data, this superiority does not hold for forecasting. The danger is especially serious when limited historical data are available.*

J. Scott Armstrong's research is a meta-analysis—it combines the results of multiple studies that address a specific hypothesis. The breakdown is as follows:

1. Eleven studies showed that complex methods outperformed simple methods

2. Twenty-one studies showed no improvement by using more complex methods

3. Seven studies showed that simple methods outperformed complex methods

Even though, on average, complex methods did not improve forecast accuracy, in fact, the performance of a more complex method in a tightly controlled research study gives an unfair and unmentioned advantage to that complex method. That is, the more complex methods perform better in a controlled research study than in a real life environment where they require more forecasting effort and maintenance.

Now that we have discussed the myth of increased model sophistication for difficult-to-forecast products, we will move into the topic of how to identify unforecastable products.

Examples of Unforecastable Demand

The central premise of this chapter is that many products are inherently unforecastable. As was stated earlier, a lack of forecastability can be determined mathematically and it can also be determined visually. I find that displaying the graphics of unforecastable products is a very educational exercise, and I have used this technique with clients to get the point across. A visual representation of unforecastability is better, in my view, than representing the same thing with a series of numbers in columns.

The following graphics are examples of unforecastable demand history. An analysis of each is provided below the screen shot.

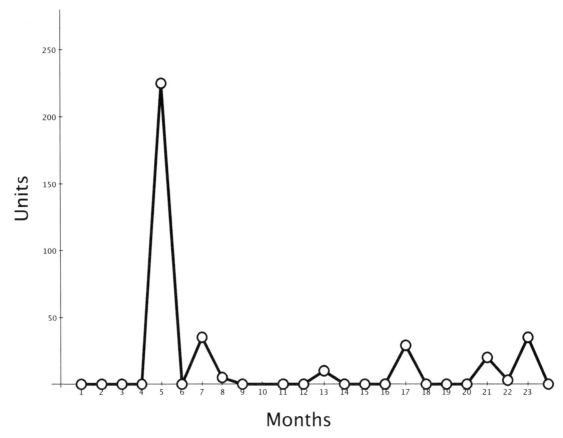

This product is clearly statistically unforecastable as there is no discernible pattern. This product has one demand peak in month seven (July), and several other smaller demand points, but simply not enough to forecast another demand point. This is a fairly obvious unforecastable demand pattern. The next example is a bit more complicated.

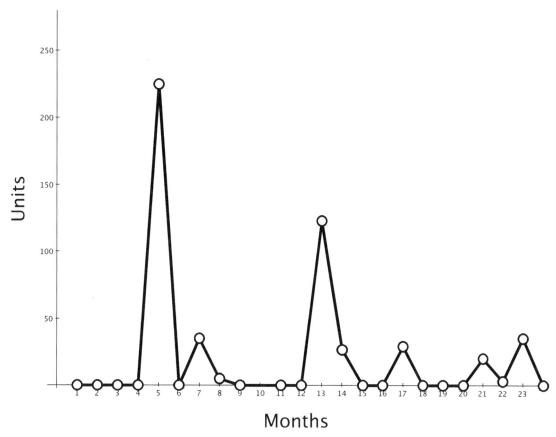

Months

In this case there are two demand peaks, and it might appear to be a good bet that the demand peak will repeat a third time...except it is not a good bet, because the first peak is in month five (May) of the first year, and the second peak is in month one, (January) in the second year. Where this product is going next is anyone's guess. This product is also unforecastable.

Lumpy Demand in JDA

While graphical analysis of forecastability is a great educational tool, it's not useful for evaluating an entire product database. For this task, usually mathematics must be performed on an extract from the system. Some vendors provide the functionality of evaluating forecastability within the application. One of these vendors is JDA.

JDA DM has an automated approach for lumpy demand identification. JDA DM flags demand that it considers too lumpy. Within their application an exception will be posted. This is called a "1013 – Irregular Demand History" exception, and can be seen in the screen shot below.

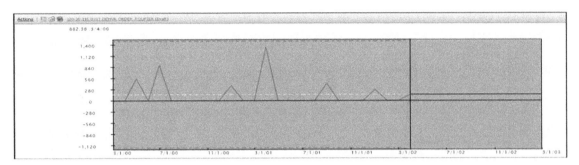

In fact, JDA DM has the concept of unforecastability built into its software, although it is not explicitly called this. The result that is produced by JDA DM is a many-period average, as is described in the quotation from JDA DM's training manual below:

> *Lumpy demand occurs when demand for a DFU is so varied that* **no pattern is distinguished**. *When the system detects lumpy demand, it will produce a one-term model with the level equal to average history.*

There are a large number of products for which no forecast can be developed that is superior to a many-period moving average or a modified many-period moving average. That is true of a purely statistical means, although judgment methods also rely at least partially upon historical pattern recognition, even if the patterns that are recognized are in the history of similar products.

Research into Methods for Dealing with Lumpy Demand

Lumpy demand is an area that has been extensively researched and for which there are many specialized forecasting algorithms. Common methods used for lumpy demand forecasting include:

1. Simple Moving Average

2. Single Exponential Smoothing

3. Croston's Method

4. SBA (Syntetos and Boylan) Method

We have already discussed the (many period) simple moving average, which is extremely simple to implement. The methods become more complex as they move from numbers one to four.

Problems with the Common Approaches for Dealing with Difficult-to-Forecast Products

The most common approach to managing difficult-to-forecast products is to put more effort into forecasting them and to attempt to forecast them with more complex algorithms. It's not as if this common approach hasn't had sufficient time to prove itself. The problems with forecasting these products are not related to limitations in mathematics or to limitations in hardware or software design that will be rectified in the future. In fact, decades ago, the hope was that more powerful computer systems would enable the automated use of more complex forecasting methods. This, of course, has not come about.

Is It Necessary to Actively Forecast the Entire Product Database?

There is no reason to hold this belief, yet it is frequently assumed to be true. More often than not, the question simply is not asked and companies forecast the entire database. Instead of taking this approach, the product database should be segmented into those product-location combinations for which active forecasting will improve the forecast, and those that will not.

How to Identify Unforecastable Products

Bill Tonetti at Demand Works has the following to say on forecastability measurement:

> *The most common estimates of "forecastability" are the coefficient of variation, which is the ratio of standard deviation divided by the series mean, and MAD-Mean ratio, which is the ration of Mean Absolute Deviation, divided by the series mean. Both of these statistics essentially do the same thing; however, the MAD-Mean ratio is superior in that it removes forecastable trends and seasonalities from the estimate by using MAD instead of SD. Smoothie, and several other applications, provide these output statistics to help companies to gauge forecastability.*

In the past I have used a formula to identify unforecastable products. The formula is placed into a spreadsheet. It can work with variables which are exported from a demand planning system. For instance, Smoothie generates a series of values that can be used as inputs to a formula that determines if products are forecastable. These values, output by the statistics file in Smoothie, include the following:

1. Series mean

2. Series Standard Deviation

3. Mean Absolute Deviation

4. Mean Absolute Percentage Error

5. R Squared

6. Model Selected (Seasonal, Level-Seasonal, Trend, etc.)

Most statistical enterprise demand planning systems can produce the identical output.

> http://www.scmfocus.com/demandplanning/2010/06/forecastable-non-forecastable-formula/

Once this analysis is complete, any company can neatly divide their product database into forecastable and unforecastable products, which can help them better manage their forecasting efforts.

Excluding Dependent Demand Products from the Analysis
In the past, when I have discussed with clients the percentage of a product database that is forecastable, the issue of dependent demand products naturally comes up. When performing the forecastability analysis, it's *unnecessary to include dependent demand products*.[7] This is because the dependent demand is easily calculated during the supply planning process. However, when a forecastability percentage is presented after the analysis is complete, it's important to explain that removing dependent demand products makes the database look much

---

[7] For those who are unfamiliar with this term, "dependent demand" means the products that depend on the demand of another product.

less forecastable than it actually is. All dependent demand products for the forecastable products are of course also forecastable.

Managing Products with No Forecast with Supply Planning

One might think that it's not really possible to simply stop forecasting products. In fact, it is quite possible and easy to implement, although there can be a fair amount of complexity in the methods designed to calculate reorder points (something that is not commonly understood by those that oppose reorder point planning on the grounds that it is too simple). In the book, *Supply Planning with MRP/DRP and APS Software,* I cover reorder point planning differently than it is covered in a number of supply planning books, so I won't repeat the information here. Suffice it to say that there are many cases where it is better not to send a forecast to the supply planning system, and the supply planning system will still manage quite well. Therefore, a simple moving average forecast can be sent for unforecastable products, or no forecast at all.

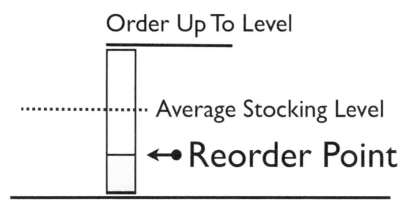

Reorder point setting does not require a forecast because the order is placed when the inventory drops to a certain level. However, there is not "one right way" of doing this. Regardless, the company gets away from continuing to invest effort in forecasting unforecastable products.

Conclusion

Analyzing the forecastability of the product database is one of the important steps to moving toward a more effective way of managing the forecasting process. For some products, a more advanced forecasting method cannot reasonably be expected to be an improvement over a simple, long duration moving average forecast. A number of trends are reducing forecastability of the product database, including actions by marketing (such as promotions) and SKU proliferation (spreading the same demand over more products). Interestingly, the connection is not frequently made between these trends and forecastability. The more erratic demand becomes, the less forecasting can add value, and increased amounts of inventory must be carried to ensure that sufficient inventory exists when demand does arrive. This fact is lost on people who are unfamiliar with forecasting.

Forecastability of the entire product database can be determined by a formula. Viewing a line graph of demand history and searching for a discernible pattern can determine forecastability of a single product or product grouping. If a pattern cannot be found visually, it is unlikely that a statistical system will be able to produce a forecast better than a level, also known as a multi-period moving average. A second category of products for which there is similarly little benefit to forecasting are those with extremely stable demand histories. Both demand histories can be set up with reorder point planning in the supply planning system.

CHAPTER 6

Accounting for Previous Promotions in Sales History

Variability in sales history results from seasonality, randomness and promotions. However, promotions are different from the normal seasonal patterns in several ways.

1. *Repeatability*: Seasonal patterns tend to repeat, and forecasting software is well designed to pick up this repetition. In fact, a specific forecasting model, called the seasonal model, is designed to do just that. On the other hand, promotions sometimes repeat, but not always. Even if there is repetition, the promotion may not occur at the same period as the previous year, or the year before that. Secondly, the size of the promotions can change. Thus it is important to develop a relationship between the size of the promotion (often meaning the price reduction) and the size of the jump in demand.

2. *One-time Events*: Many promotional events are one-time events. When looking through the sales history of many companies, these one-time events (most often uncoded promotions) can represent a very large number of units; the demand simply comes out of nowhere and then disappears again for many periods.

3. *Internal Cannibalization*: Because seasonal sales reflect true demand, they tend not to affect other parts of the product-location database. However, this is not true with promotions. Because companies now carry so many slight variations on a product, a promotion on one item can often cannibalize the sales of another product. As a result, promotions must not only be accounted for the PLC that is promoted, but also the negative sales effect of the promotions in the related PLCs. Generally this is not done in companies, meaning that promotional activities are driving variability in multiple PLCs for every one PLC that is actually put on promotion.

4. *External Cannibalization*: Furthermore, sales history is not only affected by a company's promotions, but by the promotions that are run by the company's competitors. Because promotions are so common, and because a company's competitors are often also running promotions, product sales are being altered from the actual or authentic demand by the activities of competitors that are even less likely to be accounted for in the forecasting system.

The Software for Managing Promotions

In managing promotions it's important to have the right application. Some companies use ERP systems to perform forecasting, but ERP systems lack the functionality required to effectively manage promotions. Some companies may have invested in a forecasting application already, but this is not necessarily the right or best application within which to perform promotional adjustments. Far too often companies feel compelled to use a single forecasting application, which ignores more efficient approaches for managing not only promotions, but other types of forecasting adjustments or other types of forecasting functionality. I am continually counseling my clients to not cut off their options and allow the work to get done more efficiently, and I typically receive pushback about using standard systems **rather than focusing on efficiency.** As a person who actually does all of the technical work, and who is under tight timelines, efficiency is extremely important to me. Managing promotions should not be about making the IT department happy that you are using their solution, or reinforcing past decisions made by the decision makers with respect to some approach or application selection. Instead I believe it's about using the solution that provides the best functionality for the task. In very **rare circumstances** will this be whatever the company has in-house with respect to forecasting. For instance, SAP DP (Demand Planner) is a popular forecasting application. SAP sells DP as a leading application, which it is not. I personally tune SAP DP projects and so I know the ways to improve the implementation of the application. However, one of the reasons I am successful at recovering/improving SAP DP implementations is that **I don't try** to get the application to do things that it is not good at doing. This is one of the most important rules of getting the most out of any application: don't make it do things for which it has weak functionality because of some concern that the company must use only one application in any area.

Other consultants don't have this leeway in tool selection because they work for consulting companies that are strongly aligned with SAP or they work for SAP itself. Therefore the answer must always be 100 percent SAP. However, promotional planning is onerous in SAP DP. This is not to say that promotions **cannot be** entered into SAP DP; that can be easily done, but SAP DP is not a good environment for the identification and adjustment of outliers. Additionally, once promotional sales are accounted for in any system, it's important to be able to see that reflected in both the model selected as well as the forecastability measurements. However, running the best-fit procedure in DP traditionally consumes a lot of resources, and the forecastability figures do not immediately update when the promotional adjustments are made. Finally, SAP DP is not a fully capable attribute-based forecasting system. I say this because attributes cannot be easily changed and then added to the interface for navigation purposes. It is expensive and time-consuming to adjust the hierarchy in SAP DP, which is why most companies only do it occasionally. Furthermore, once created, navigation within SAP DP is cumbersome, and does not allow users to flexibly group the PLCs that a user may need to group, providing statistics on any group the user chooses to select.

Therefore, I find it far more preferable to create the adjustments to the resultant history in an external application and then upload the new history to SAP DP.

I can't emphasize this enough: the system must serve the task at hand. The user or analyst does not exist to serve the system. At least logically, this should not be the case; however, I have worked with many IT departments that, while they would never come out and say it, clearly operated from the perspective that the business exists to serve the interests of the system—or more broadly, the interests of IT. So in the strongest possible terms, do not use whatever application is sitting around that the company purchased for who knows what reason. Get the budget to use the right tool for the job; it will easily pay for itself in reduced man-hours and in better outcomes. In fact, one of the reasons that companies have such problems managing promotions is, in addition to not knowing how to do it; they have inappropriate tools for the job. Most companies believe they need to use only one application for every area. However, I can say definitively that this is an unsubstantiated belief. Here are several reasons why a company may need to rely on more than one application in any area.

1. *Variety of Functionality:* Different applications have different strengths and weaknesses.

2. *Different Degrees of Use:* Using an application does not mean that it must be fully implemented. There are many applications that can be purchased and their functionality leveraged at a reasonable price, without actually implementing them as the main live system. I know, because I do this all the time when I simulate demand, supply and production planning for companies in the applications that I own.

3. *The False Logic of Getting More from One Application:* Research performed at Software Decisions[1] comparing TCO estimation across multiple application categories shows that only about 10 percent of an application's TCO is related to its software cost. Therefore, the fact that a company "already owns" software is not a substantial argument for why it should use an application that has weak functionality in a particular area. As SaaS becomes increasingly prevalent, enterprise software will move towards incremental pricing, and under this scenario, using multiple applications will become even more appealing than it is currently. IT departments that are interested in controlling the access of business to functionality and that is debating how everyone must use "one system" will be left out as this occurs.

---

[1] http://www.softwaredecisions.org

With all of this in mind, let's review the criteria by which a forecasting software application should be measured with regards to its suitability for managing promotions.

1. *Outliers Management:* The application must be able to quickly and easily identify outliers from an overall database of PLCs, and this outlier configuration must be easy to change.

2. *Forecastability:* Once the adjustment to the promotion is made, the result should be calculated immediately and viewable within the application so the effect of the promotional adjustment can be viewed.

3. *Grouping/Attributes:* The application must provide flexible grouping and must be fully attribute-capable, which means it must be adjustable by the user with no input from IT. If IT is required to make these adjustments, they will not be made in a timely fashion, and IT will begin to interfere with the project in others ways (e.g., offering their opinions on how the work should be done). We want IT out of the way, and attribute adjustment is critical to the process because the attributes that must be built will not already be in the forecasting system.
   a. New attributes should be easy to add to the PLCs database.
   b. If one wants to select any grouping, either by attribute or by any manual selection, the forecasting application should show all statistics and model selection by **that** group.

4. *Best-fit Procedure:* Once the promotional adjustment is made, it can sometimes mean a change to the model that is assigned by the best-fit procedure. However, in order for this to happen, it is necessary for the best-fit procedure to run immediately after the change is made. This will then show the user what happens to the forecasting method applied based upon the promotional adjustments. Promotions that are unaccounted for confuse the best-fit procedure; adjusting for the promotion will often cause the forecasting application to switch to a new forecasting model.
   a. Best-fit functionality is not created equal in all forecasting applications.
   b. Best-fit functionality must be measured on much more than simply the ability of its mathematics to pick the best model.
   c. It's quite common for software vendors to include best-fit function-

ality, but it is something else to make the functionality easy to use and to fit it naturally into how the application works.

5. *Graphical Capabilities:* Good graphics make any forecasting job easier. However, they are critical for the part of the process that requires getting input from Sales/Marketing as to which outliers are promotions, and what percentage of the outliers should be considered related to the promotion. This is the fourth step of the **Promotion Identification and Update** process that is explained later in this chapter. Sales/Marketing must be able to clearly see the magnitude of the outlier as this greatly speeds up the process of jogging their memory, produces faster and better recall, and makes the overall process run much more smoothly.

One of the major reasons that companies have problems with accounting for promotions in their forecasting systems is that their forecasting systems do not perform these functions. This is the advantage I have when I come to a new client: I bring my own software that I have selected, and I am not bound by the software that the company has selected.

Porting the Promotional Changes to the Live System
In addition to what was just covered, promotional adjustments are imported into the production forecasting system. Ordinarily this is quite simple to do. In systems that cannot hold multiple histories, such as with many ERP systems, the Resultant History (which is the Actual History plus or minus the adjustments) can be uploaded from the promotion adjustment system to the ERP system. If there is not a place to hold this information, it must overwrite the Actual History. Without customization (which should be avoided) the ERP system is no longer the system of record for sales history, assuming that it is currently.[2] This is not actually a problem, and in fact, although ERP software vendors often propose that the ERP system must be or should be the system of record, often it is not feasible. It's simply a power play by ERP systems vendors to be at the center of the company's universe to increase their control over the account. IBM was the first company in hardware and software to perfect

---

[2] For those unfamiliar with the term, the "system of record" is essentially the "horse's mouth" on the topic of data. It is the system where the data is maintained and which updates other systems.

account control; this is where you develop your overall strategy combined with misinforming your client in order to get them to perpetually choose your offering. ERP software vendors have been applying similar account control since ERP systems were first introduced in the mid-1980s.[3] [4]

Following the "account control rule" rather than any computer science rule, ERP software vendors propose they are the system of record in all cases. However, **no system** that has **less functionality** in the same area as another system that the company uses can be the system of record.[5] If one system has more fields on a particular topic than another system, then the system with more fields must be the system of record. Therefore, if the ERP system can hold one version of the sales history, but an external forecasting system can hold multiple versions of history (as well as many other fields related to forecasting) then the external forecasting system is actually the system of record, and the ERP system simply becomes a customer of the external forecasting system.

---

[3] A good example of account control is explained in this quotation: *"Unfortunately, IT really doesn't like blended vendors and tends to prefer as homogenous a shop as it can to lower problems with service. If vendors could just come in and sell the high-margin stuff, most would have abandoned the lower-margin commodity servers long ago. This also goes to account control because if you can't contain the entire shop, or most of it, you won't be the primary vendor and secondary vendors are typically easier to displace. In short, if you have IBM and Oracle in a shop and IBM can provide all of the IT needs but Oracle is picking and choosing, over time, IBM should be able to displace Oracle because it can fight on more fronts and increasingly structure deals to require hardware Oracle doesn't want to provide or increasingly no longer sells."* – How Oracle Is Giving Up Account Control to IBM

[4] ERP and account control are covered in my book *The Real Story Behind ERP: Separating Fiction from Reality*.

[5] Some ERP software vendors that have very limited functionality in many areas do attempt to convince their customers that their software should be the system of record for all data. However, if the ERP system lacks many of the fields that exist in legacy or in an external system, how can this be the case? The ERP vendor will sometimes argue that these fields should be simply added—or customized—so that they exist within the ERP system. This makes very little sense as these fields simply become placeholders within the ERP system. Fields are supposed to actually drive functionality. Where the entire system of record issue becomes very problematic is in the area of bill of materials management. As I cover in the book *The Bill of Materials in Excel, Planning, ERP and BMMS/PLM Systems*, ERP systems should never be the system of record for BOM information.

This issue is repeated in every application area; ERP systems will always have fewer fields because they have less functionality in a particular area than an application that specializes in that area. Yet decision makers continue to accept claims from ERP vendors that the ERP system is the system of record for all data.

Sophisticated Promotions Management for Forecasting

This section combines the topic of system adjustments with the results of academic research in the area of promotional adjustments. The academic research is mixed on the effect of promotions; so much of a promotion's success depends upon how the promotion was run. What is known is that the results of a promotion are more complicated than simply an examination of the immediate effect. Any promotion will of course have an effect on the number of units sold because a reduced price changes the desirability of an item, and while a promotion is often discussed as having only one impact— the initial effect on the number of units sold in the promotional period— it actually has effects in both the short and long term:

1. *Following Period Effects (Short Term):* Because a promotion will only partially change the actual pattern of consumption, promotions will lead to reductions in demand in the period or periods following the promotion.

2. *Following Period Effects (Long Term):* Promotions can have long-term effects on consumption, but these effects are much smaller than either the initial or short-term effects, and are much more difficult to model. The cost of modeling them is also relatively high.

Promotions must be accounted for in the demand history because they are artificial adjustments to demand. The conclusion I have come to through work and research is that most companies do **not** account for previous promotions in their demand history. When discussing this topic with IT, I find that sometimes the information regarding the history of promotions is likely somewhere in some system, but has not actually been correlated to demand history. Therefore the statistical forecasting models that are used by companies will reproduce promotional effects in periods where there are no promotions planned, or the average forecast will simply be lifted for all months, even though the promotion may have only occurred in one or two months.

For instance, SAP ERP does not have promotion forecasting functionality, so even if the promotion periods were identified there is no way short of either directly adjusting the demand history or customizing the system to incorporate promotional periods/flags into SAP ERP.[6] In fact, the more one studies promotions, the more startling the many implications promotions have in different areas become, and the clearer the necessity to account for promotions properly becomes.

The Promotion Adjustment Calculator

One tool that could be developed to enable sales and marketing to better leverage their market intelligence is what I refer to as a Promotion Adjustment Calculator or PAC. The PAC estimates the change in demand relative to price changes. When sales and marketing provides input to forecasting as to how much of a previous month of demand was attributable to a promotion, or how much the forecast should be increased in relation to a promotion, this is really just an informal estimate of what a PAC does more formally.

The PAC is based upon historical changes in demand due to previous promotions associated with product categories. An example of the logic of such a tool is shown in the following graphic:

---

[6] Some of the online documentation from SAP on this topic is confusing, even to a person with many years of SAP experience in both SAP ERP and SAP APO. When SAP discusses promotion management in their online documentation, SAP is actually referring to SAP DP—an entirely different system and not part of SAP (ERP) ECC, but part of the SAP APO advanced planning suite, which has enhanced forecasting functionality. SAP documentation will describe functionality, but will sometimes leave out what application is **actually** being described.

Promotion Adjustment Calculator

Product Category	Product	Percent Price Decrease	Relationship	Intial Forecast in Cases	Quantity Increase Due to Promotion
A	Tuna Fish	15%	1.5% Change in Volume Per 1% Change in Price	2,000	450
A	Macrel	10%	1.5% Change in Volume Per 1% Change in Price	3,200	480
B	Pineapple Juice	2%	2.7% Change in Volume Per 1% Change in Price	300	16
B	Orange Drink with Ginger	6%	2.7% Change in Volume Per 1% Change in Price	450	73

Analysis of previous promotions and other price adjustments would allow for the creation of a Promotion Adjustment Calculator for future promotions and price adjustments. This would take the guesswork out of promotional adjustments and allow a more accurate and consistent application of promotional forecast adjustments.

The Application of Promotion Forecast Adjustments

However, determination of how much to adjust the forecast is not the end of the story. After the promotional adjustment is determined, one must make the adjustment. Exactly how this adjustment is made is important. The adjustments should meet the following criteria:

1. *Ease of Use:* The adjustment should be easy to apply, both to individual items as well as to aggregated items. This is important for time management and also for reasons of quality, as explained in the following quotation. *"Biased forecasts can be caused by inconsistencies in judgment that occur when large numbers of forecasts are produced or adjusted using qualitative techniques. The repetition inherent in these multiple forecasts encourages boredom which leads to inconsistent and inaccurate forecasts."* – Sales Forecasting Management

2. *Aggregated Changes:* One example of the overall principle of the first point. One should be able to make the changes on a single product or a single product location, and on a combination of attributes (location being one example of an attribute), and on the basis of any aggregation

that is necessary in order to quickly and consistently apply promotional adjustments. In fact, products could be categorized by their promotion category (which would be determined by their increase versus price changes), as is determined by the PAC as explained above, and have promotional adjustments made as an aggregate.

3. *Long-Term Recording and Effect on Demand History:* The adjustment should be traceable within the system so that it is recorded specifically as a promotional adjustment and not some other type of adjustment. This is because a promotion is not a **normal** forecast adjustment and has important implications for how the demand history should be treated by the forecasting system after the demand for the forecast period passes. Currently, at many companies, promotional forecast adjustments are made the same way that non-promotional adjustments are made.

4. *Shareability:* Everyone should be able to see the direct changes made, for instance in a planning meeting.

In most forecasting applications, there is a specific promotions row. The promotional "boost" is then entered separately from the forecast itself. How this is done is shown in the following screen shot.

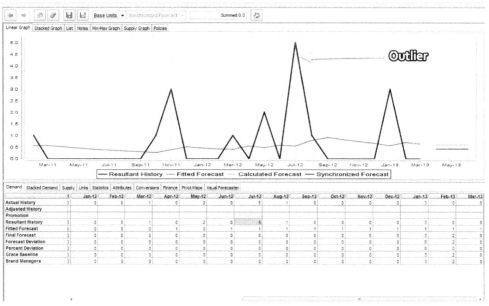

This is the before screen shot above. In this step we have found an outlier, and we have spoken to Sales/Marketing and determined that this was due to a promotion. We have been told that the estimated promotional amount was four units.

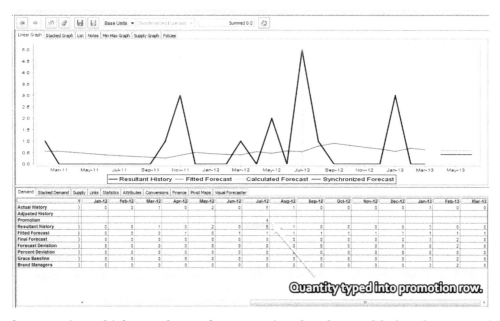

Now the quantity, which was due to the promotion, has been added to the system by typing it directly into the user interface. However, the forecast has not yet been recalculated.

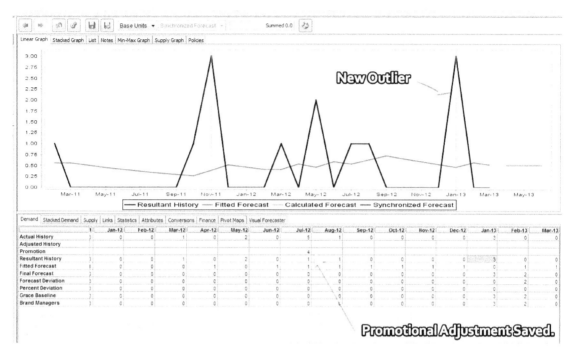

Notice that the Resultant History has declined to one unit because the effect of the promotion on the sales history has been removed. The forecast is based upon the Resultant History, not the Actual History. The Resultant History = the Actual History +/- any adjustments. This is important because in forecasting, the forecast **should not** be driven off of Actual History—and this is a perfect example of why.

Notice that the largest outlier has also adjusted in the graph, and the next step is to evaluate other outliers. The outlier is determined by the user in the model setup, and any historical data point that is outside of the threshold set in the application receives a highlighted (red for those with the electronic version of this book) square. This allows the user to focus in on that data point.

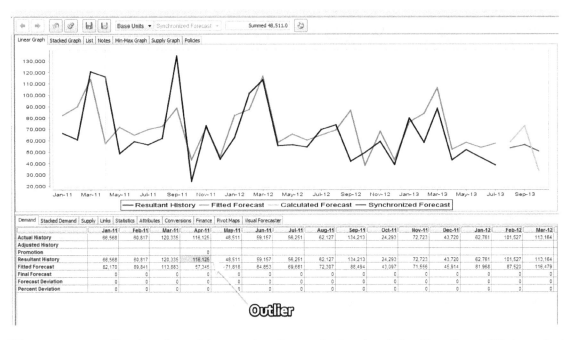

The way an outlier is selected is not simply on the basis of the Resultant History, but on the relationship between the Resultant History and the Fitted Forecast. The Fitted Forecast is what the forecasting system predicted the sales would be, based upon the model that has been selected. This PLC is a perfect example of this; notice that the Resultant History for March is 120,335 units, which is higher than the Resultant History for April. However, **April is marked as an outlier**, because the forecast for March was 113,883 units while the forecast for April was 57,345 units. Therefore, it is the discrepancy between the Resultant History and the Fitted Forecast —combined with the setting in terms of the standard deviation of demand—that makes a Resultant History data point an outlier.

Behind the scenes, this forecasting application will create the forecast for the upwardly adjusted quantity, but it will be recorded as a promotional quantity and period. This is explained in the following quotation from the application's developer, Demand Works:

> "Historic promotions values are automatically **deducted** from Actual History to produce a baseline forecast. Future promotions are **added** automatically to the calculated forecast."

This means that the statistical forecasting method used will only look at the promotion-deducted Actual History to produce the forecast, and will not be fooled into replicating a higher forecast if no promotion exists in the future forecasted period.

Aggregated Promotional Adjustments

This previous example was simple; it was a promotional adjustment on a single product. But what if a promotion applies to a group of products? It can be tedious to enter the promotional adjustment one PLC at a time, and the efficiency of applying promotion adjustments is important. However, with the right functionality it is not always necessary to make promotional adjustments one by one, or to make promotional adjustments in a spreadsheet and then upload the adjustments into the forecasting application. This is explained in the following quotation from Demand Works:

> *"Promotions can be input on any base-level item, or they may be input on any aggregated node (group of items). When inputting promotions on an aggregate node, you will be prompted as to whether **you would like the promotions quantities to be allocated to the items in that group**."*

Following Period Promotional Adjustment

Up to this point we have not addressed the issue of the promotional adjustment in the **periods following the period with the promotion**. As promotions only partially adjust actual consumption (that is, if tuna fish is reduced in price, people may substitute tuna fish for swordfish in their diet), some of what occurs in promotions is stockpiling.[7] This is explained in the following quotation from a paper on the topic of stockpiling:

> *"In contrast, a long-term effect refers to the cumulative effect of previous promotional exposures on a consumer's current, or short-*

---

[7] Stockpiling is well documented in the academic literature, but amusingly, there is a website called Stockpiling Moms that provides guidance on how to shop on sales (promotions) and how to stockpile from these events to lower one's food bill. http://www.stockpilingmoms.com/getting-started/stockpiling-101-series/

term decision of whether and how much to buy. The effect of past exposures on current purchases also suggests a carryover effect; a promotion in the current period will affect behavior in subsequent periods."

– The Long Term Impact of Promotions in
Consumer Stockpiling Behavior

According to research published in the *Journal of Marketing Research* in 2007, the following changes to consumption and stockpiling were observed in their study:

1. *Yogurt*: Extra consumption accounted for between 49 and 65 percent of the promotional bump.

2. *Ketchup*: Extra consumption accounted for between 30 and 58 percent of the promotional bump.

In fact, the literature on promotions and their effect on consumer behavior is quite interesting. I have included several quotations in this book, but a full review of the research into the promotional effect on consumer behavior is tangential to the treatment of promotions in this book—which is simply that they are part of the equation to be more effectively modeled by companies in order to capture higher forecast accuracy.[8] If the changes to demand volume in the post-promotion period are not accounted for, the statistical forecasting method that is used by the system will overestimate the demand of the months following the promotion period.

Making Promotional Adjustments in the Application

How much the promotional forecast should be adjusted in the following periods depends upon how much consumers either alter their consumption or simply stockpile. This can be determined by analyzing the demand history.

---

[8] *"Promotions erode purchasing probabilities by lowering reference prices and thereby increasing price sensitivity. As a result consumers might be more reluctant to pay regular prices or tolerate price increases. Such arguments are consistent with a lie-in-wait strategy, in which consumers are less likely to buy at high prices as they learn to buy when prices are low."* – The Long Term Impact of Promotions in Consumer Stockpiling Behavior

To illustrate how this works, I have put together an example. In the following example we have a "100 percent stockpile scenario," where the customers simply move their purchases forward by a month in response to the promotion but do not at all **alter** their consumption. How this scenario—which can accept promotional adjustments—would be accounted for in an application is illustrated below.

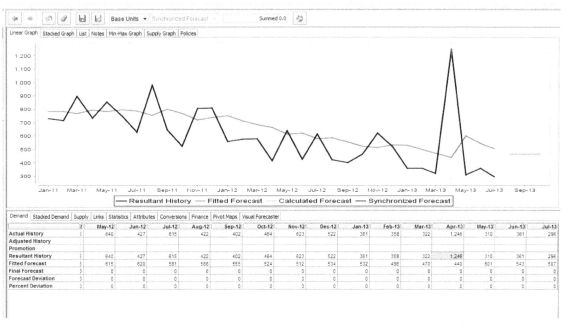

Here we have an outlier that we determined was due to a promotion, just as we have covered up to this point. However, in this case I will make another adjustment that will account for the change in demand that followed the promotion.

The research into promotional effects on demand indicate that it is more likely that some combination of **consumption increase and stockpiling will occur**—and it is likely that it will occur in more than one of the following periods. However, let's keep this adjustment simple by only making an additional adjustment to the period that immediately follows the promotional period. For this company we estimate that any promotion will lead to a reduction in sales in the following month of one-fourth the consumption of the promotional month. This is to account for stockpiling. Therefore, 75 percent of the effect of the promotion is to cause increased consumption in the month of the promotion, while 25 percent of the effect is related to stockpiling (buyers purchasing a month before they actually use the item). We can model this in the forecasting system in the following way.

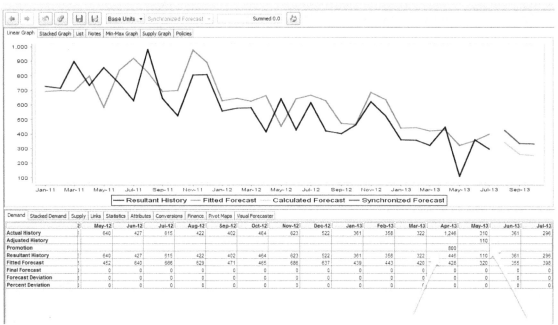

Now we have inserted a positive 800 units for April, and a negative adjustment to the history in May of 25% * 800 or 200 units. We needed to subtract 200 units from the Actual History (310 units), which results in 110 units. This is what we will enter as the Actual History. Once we saved the changes, the database was updated. And we have now accounted for the promotional effect—not only in the promotional month, but in the following month as well.

The above is a hypothetical example to demonstrate a principle. Actual values would require data analysis per product, or more likely per product group as a specific per-product analysis would be quite time-consuming. There would also be a trade-off between accuracy and modeling effort; increasing the number of product groups may increase accuracy, but there will be a **diminishing utility versus the analytical cost** to create the new product groups.

The Promotional Effects on Brand Switching

It should also be observed that this previous example does not represent all of the effects of promotions. Another effect is the ability of a promotion to get customers to switch to the promoted brand from another brand (which is, of course, another purpose of the promotion). However, the *Journal of Marketing Research* article "Decomposition of the Sales Impact of Promotion-Induced Stockpiling" found this effect to be **small for some items, and medium in their effect but difficult to estimate for others**. For instance, they estimated this effect to be between 2 and 3 percent in yogurt and between 3 and 16 percent in ketchup. Note that these values were taken from a research study to illustrate the principle; companies should not apply these values to their own business and promotions (not even food companies). Instead, each company should analyze its own demand and promotion history.

Promotions and Fake Seasonality

Best-fit forecasting is explained in the term section in Chapter 1, "Introduction." Best fit matches the forecast method to the PLC on the basis of the demand history. In testing forecasting databases for a number of companies, it is quite common to find a "fake" seasonal pattern. When a forecasting system picks up a seasonal pattern, it will apply a seasonal forecasting model and attempt to reproduce seasonality into the future.

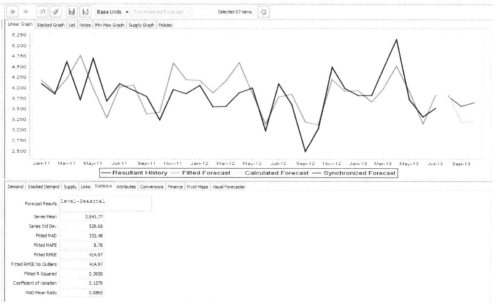

This is a selection of a number of PLCs. As can be seen from the graphic above, as well as looking at the model selection field (which shows a Level-Seasonal forecasting model

selected—which means the combined sales history of the selected PLCs has compo-
nents of level and seasonality). What can often happen is that promotions, which often
repeat, are picked up as seasonality by the best-fit procedure of the forecasting system.
Often seasonality is caused by authentic customer demand, but it can be inserted into
demand history artificially through things like promotions.

This finding is not at all uncommon. If promotions are not accounted for in the demand history, promotions may often be interpreted as a seasonal pattern of demand due to the quarterly timing of promotions. A seasonal pattern is simply a repeating series of demand changes; however, the details depend upon the particular scenario, one of which is described in the following quotation.

> *"We actually worked with one company that explained to us its*
> *unique 'quarterly seasonal pattern.' The pattern clearly showed that*
> *sales always were high in the first two months of each quarter and*
> *low in the third month. The pattern repeated each quarter, and the*
> *company wanted to know what would cause its customers to buy in*
> *such a way. Upon investigation, we found that sales quotas (which*
> *were based on sales forecasts) actually were set too low, and the*
> *salespeople received lower commissions for any sales in excess of the*
> *quota in any quarter. Thus members of the sales force simply sold*
> *at normal levels until their quota was met and would not call on*
> *customers during the third month. Of course this caused considerable*
> *production and logistics costs to address this 'seasonal' pattern."*
> — Sales Forecasting Management

Unaccounted-for Promotional Sales and Best-fit Forecasting

Promotional sales that are not accounted for are damaging to forecasting. Promotional sales that are unaccounted for interfere with forecast model selection. The best-fit procedure cannot work properly if the previous promotions look like **authentic demand to the** forecasting system, and I provide an example of this in the following screen shot. These screen shots show how damaging unaccounted-for outliers are when one is attempting to perform best-fit model selection.

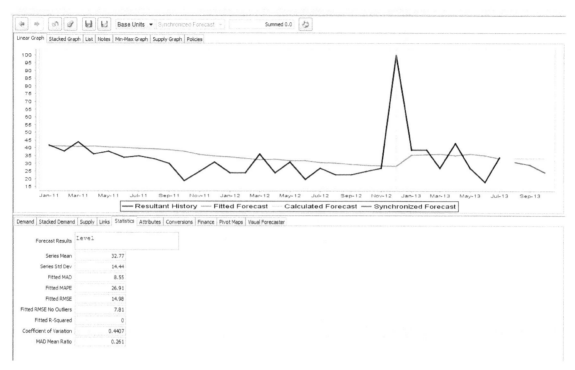

Here we have a large outlier. The best-fit procedure has selected a Level forecast method because it cannot find a pattern to the sales history.[9] The forecasting system has also assigned a Fitted R-Square of zero. This is how we know (although we can also tell by the graph) that the best-fit procedure that was run on this item was not able to find a pattern to the sales history that it thinks can be relied upon to produce a forecast. Zero is the lowest value any data set can attain in terms of forecastability. However, we have a very large outlier, which is degrading our forecast statistics.

---

[9] This application uses the term "Level." The more common term is a "constant forecast."

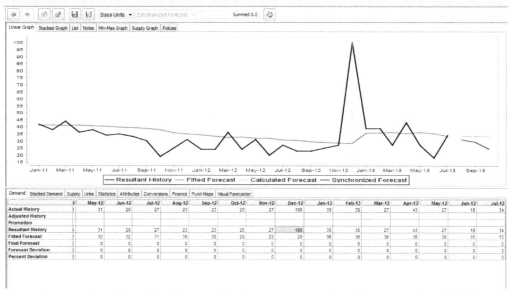

When we change the tab to the Demand tab we can see that the quantity of 100 units in December has been flagged as an outlier. We currently have the outliers set to two standard deviations away from the mean, and this is entirely controllable in the settings of the application. Outliers are flagged in the Resultant History, and not in the Actual History. Any adjustment that is made will have no impact on the Actual History, but only on the Resultant History.

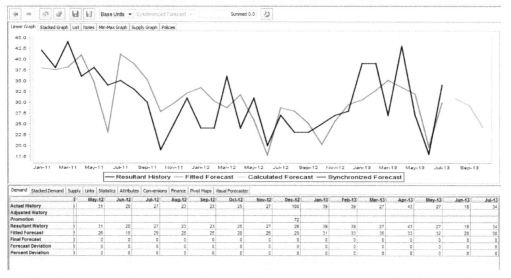

This outlier happens to be a promotion, and we want to account for this outlier so that the forecasting system does not think this was authentic demand. We adjust the Re-

sultant History (the history the forecast is based upon) by adding 72 units to the Promotions row for December. We arrive at 72 units based upon an estimate of the sales increase that was driven by the price change from using a Promotion Adjustment Calculator, which was discussed previously. The promotion value now decrements from the Actual History and the Resultant History now only shows sales of 28. Notice that once this change is saved, the overall graph changes, and a pattern emerges. This pattern was hidden previously because the graph had to scale upward to show the outlier.

Accounting for the promotion had a number of impacts on this PLC. First, notice that the forecast model changed from a Level to a Level-Seasonal. When I saved the change to promotions, the best-fit procedure ran for this PLC and a new model was selected. Just as with the graph, where the smaller pattern was hidden from view, the same is true for the best-fit procedure, which could not pick up the smaller authentic pattern because of the outlier. If we review the statistics we can see that the fitted MAPE is now smaller at 17.53 whereas previously it was 26.91, which is a predicted accuracy improvement of almost 10 percentage points. Secondly, the Fitted-R-Square has improved from zero to .34, meaning that this PLC is now far more forecastable than it was. We are not simply removing data points in order to improve our forecast statistics; that would be called overfitting. Instead we are accounting for an outlier that was driven by an artificial input (that is the promotion) that was not part of authentic demand.

Finding and Accounting for Promotions in the Sales History

Many companies believe that inserting their promotional history into their forecasting system is quite onerous, and therefore they don't do it. However, I have found a very efficient way to locate promotions and if you have the right software, it is actually quite simple. How much actual work is involved depends upon a combination of how many PLCs the company has, and how many outliers the company has on average per PLC. The steps for updating the sales history with promotions are listed below:

1. Determine the Outlier Threshold

2. Set Up the Outlier Threshold in the System

3. Filter Outliers to Obtain the PLCs to be Evaluated

4. Meet with Sales/Marketing to Obtain Input on Promotions

5. Build the PAC Through the Process of Working with Sales/Marketing

6. Update the Forecasting System with the Adjusted History

Step 1—Determine the Outlier Threshold

The "correct" setting for the outlier threshold depends upon the magnitude of the promotion's effect on sales. If a company runs promotions that result in smaller changes to sales, then it would make sense to bring down the standard deviations. The intent is to set the outlier threshold to catch all the promotions. The outlier threshold determines how broadly or narrowly the net is set, and how many "fish" will be caught by the "net."

Step 2—Set Up the Outlier Threshold in the System

To identify outliers, first set up the threshold by which a data point is flagged as an outlier. In the application I am using for this book, Smoothie, the outlier threshold is set up in the Model Options, as you can see in the following screen shot.

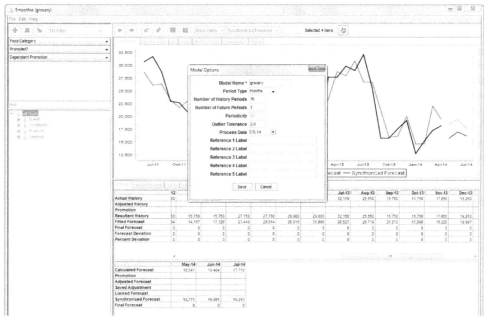

In Smoothie, two standard deviations is the default value. When set to two standard deviations, it captures anything greater than two standard deviations from the mean. That means that the outlier is identified when it is outside of 95.4 percent of expected value of the time series.

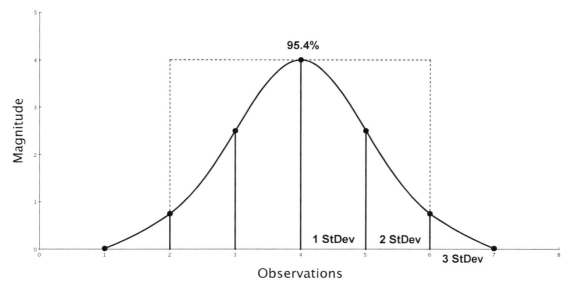

Two standard deviations leave all of the values that are 2.3 percent on each side of the normal distribution curve.

This variance is **not** between the various sales history data points, but is the standard deviation of the variance between the Fitted Forecast and the Resultant History. If we think about it logically, if the average of the time series is 100 units, and we find a month with sales of 300 units, that may seem high, but if the forecast was 270, then there is no reason to tag it as an outlier.[10] It's easy to fall into the thought pattern of assuming that the outlier is simply the sales level versus the mean sales value, but that is not how the outlier is calculated.

Step 3—Filter Outliers to Obtain the PLCs to be Evaluated

The next step is to filter the PLC database by outliers. In Smoothie this is a default filter, and as soon as I select it, I will only see the PLCs that **have at least one outlier**. Now they may have any number higher than one outlier, but the rule is that any PLC with an outlier needs to be reviewed. Some exceptions to this would be a category of the PLC database that never goes on promotion, and therefore, any outliers in this category do not require analysis. There is an easy way to handle that: I can either create a custom filter or I can create a navigational attribute, and this will create a hierarchy that I can select. I can then run this filter while I select the category/grouping of PLCs that does go out on promotion.

---

[10] While we have been focusing on positive outliers, the standard deviation works in both directions—that is, both sides of the normal distribution curve—so very low values will also be flagged as outliers.

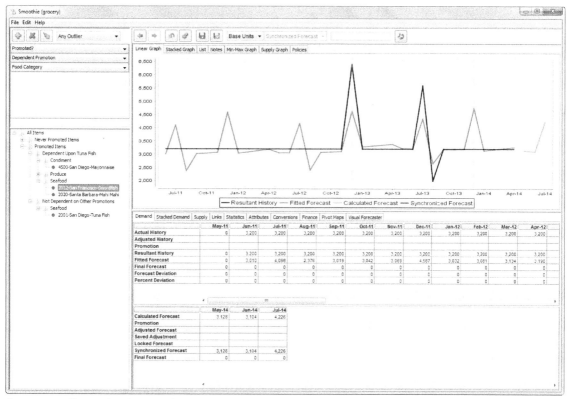

I can easily code the PLC database for those product location combinations that actively have promotions run for them. That will save time by eliminating the need to go through a number of PLCs whose outliers are not promotionally driven.

Notice the hierarchy to the left. This hierarchy was created to both explain and simplify the process of managing promotions. I have selected Swordfish, which is under the attribute/hierarchy of "Promoted Items."

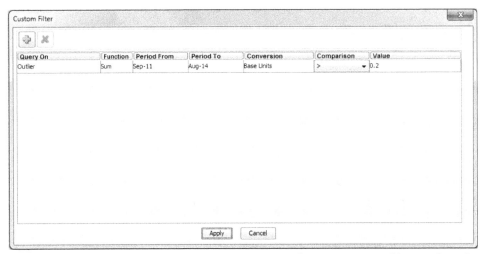

Some of the PLCs in this list have promotions, and some are outliers related to other things. Each outlier must be analyzed on a case-by-case basis.

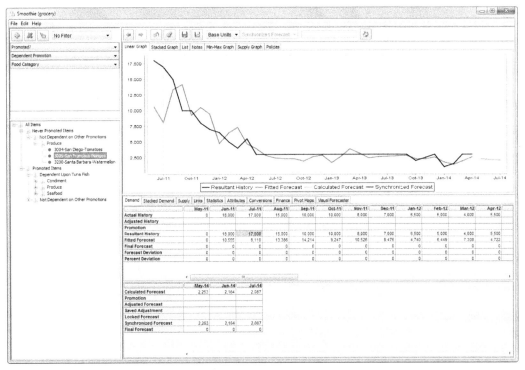

Here I have selected a PLC that is under the attribute/hierarchy called "Never Promoted Items." Therefore, when I run the outlier filter, I do so without selecting this attribute/hierarchy. This saves a great deal of time.

After having analyzed the sales history data of quite a few companies, when the outlier threshold is set to two standard deviations or more, there typically end up being **not that many** outliers per PLC. Promotions are very important to include in the forecast, but the beneficial aspect of identification and adjustment is that there are not that many of them per PLC (although quite a few in aggregate), making the task of going through and finding and coding the history of promotions less of a chore than many companies seem to imagine. This is explained by the following quotation.

> *"...in our experience, even the most frequently promoted articles are not going to have more than a dozen promotions in their market lifetime. In average, the amount of past known promotions for a given article is ridiculously low, ranging from zero to one past promotion in average. As a result, you can't expect any reliable results by focusing on the past promotions a single product at a time, because, most of the time there isn't any."*
>
> – Better Forecasts in Retail

This quotation also highlights that it is often necessary to use promotion samples from multiple products to forecast a future promotion, due to the limited sample available from one specific product.

Step 4—Meet with Sales/Marketing to Receive Input on Promotions

At this point, with the filtered set of PLCs that contain outliers, it is time to meet with Sales/Marketing. I have found that this is best accomplished by meeting in a room and projecting the forecasting application on an overhead projector, and getting feedback. Sales/Marketing can then provide their insights as to whether the outlier is in fact a promotion, and how many of the outliers were related to the promotion. The forecasting database can have the promotion quantity added to the promotion row right on the spot. Having gone through this exercise several times, Sales/Marketing does tend to know which outliers are promotions when they are shown the outliers in a good quality graphical environment. This is another reason the application chosen should have good graphical capabilities.

After all promotions have been accounted for, it is beneficial to produce a report showing how much more forecastable the PLC database has become post-promotion adjustment. While this will always be the case, most decision makers within companies are not aware of this fact. This can be accomplished by taking screen shots of the forecastability statistics within the application before and after the promotional adjustments, and then providing a brief overview of the concept of forecastability. This will help the company understand how they will likely benefit from the work, as it will take some time for the company to see the improvements from increased forecast accuracy. Furthermore, it helps in the future to document the effort and allow others to understand what was done.

Step 5—Build the PAC Through the Process of Working with Sales/Marketing

Every data point provided by Sales/Marketing regarding the effect of a previous promotion on demand is a data point that should be recorded and used to build the PAC, which is then used for forecasting promotions. This step supports this process and also the process of making adjustments to forecasts (covered in Chapter 7, "Adding Promotions into the Forecast").

The next step is sharing this new data with other systems.

Step 6—Update Forecasting System with the Adjusted History

As I said previously, it is not necessary and often it is not desirable to manage promotions using the same forecasting system that is currently used for other forecasting tasks. What **is** necessary is to update the live forecasting system with the updates from the promotion identification and adjustment process. As we have covered up to this point, just the promotions can be uploaded if the production forecasting system has a promotions row, and it works to adjust whatever the application calls the Resultant History. If the system does not have something like Resultant/Adjusted History, the "Actual History" can be overwritten with the Resultant History from this exercise.

Show Promotional Adjustment from Cannibalization

Because promotions often cause cannibalization of one's own products, it is necessary to account for this cannibalization by placing a **negative** promotional quantity on the affected PLCs. In order to do this effectively, some relationship must be developed between the increase in sales from one PLC and a corresponding decrease in the sales of another PLC. This can be viewed as just a **modified** Promotion Adjustment Calculator (PAC) that we covered earlier.

Promotion Adjustment Calculator

Product Category	Product	Percent Price Decrease	Relationship	Intial Forecast in Cases	Quantity Increase Due to Promotion
A	Tuna Fish	15%	(positive)8% Change in Volume Per 1% Change in Price	2,000	2,400
A	Swordfish	0%	(negative) 1.1% Change in Volume Per 1% Change in **Price of Tuna Fish**	3,200	(528.00)
A	Mahi Mahi	0%	(negative) 2.7% Change in Volume Per 1% Change in **Price of Tuna Fish**	300	(121.50)

*This is very similar to the previous PAC that we covered, except this time the cannibalized PLCs have a **negative** relationship with the promotion of another PLC. Now we will go in and make these adjustments to the promotion row for the PLCs above within the forecasting application. This means that three adjustments to the PLC database must be made. As well, these changes must also be made when planning for future promotions (the topic of Chapter 7).*

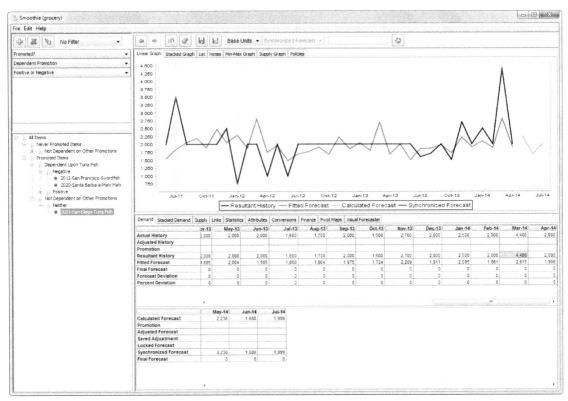

Here I have selected the Promoted Item/Not Dependent Upon Other Promotions attribute/hierarchy. This is Tuna Fish. The highlighted cell of Resultant History in March shows an outlier of 4,400 units. Based upon our PAC, we estimate that 2,400 units of the 4,400 units were due to the promotion that was run in that month. Therefore, we need to add 2,400 as the quantity that is attributable to the promotion.

Now we enter 2,400 in the promotion row, and then save the change so it updates the database. Our Resultant History is now 2,000 instead of 4,400. However, some of the demand is reduced from other products that the company carries through the process of substitution, which is explained the PAC above.

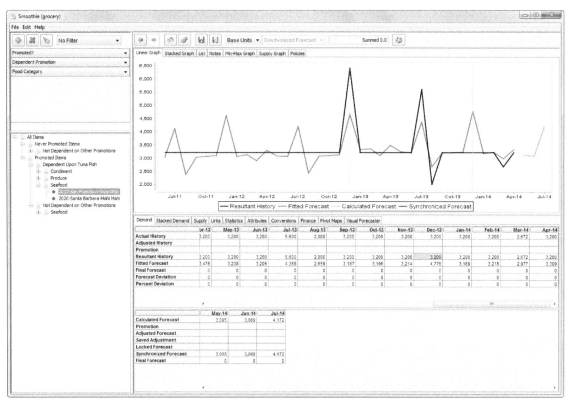

*Here is swordfish, which is one of the PLCs for which demand declines when a pro-
motion is run on Tuna Fish. An outlier is selected in December, but that does not have
anything to do with the adjustment we are about to make. Instead we need to focus attention on the month of March. Notice that the sales history for March for Sword Fish
was down from the previous month and the following month. Our PAC tells us that we
need to provide a **negative** promotion adjustment.*

A **positive** promotion adjustment means that we are telling the forecast system that some of the sales were attributed to a promotion and were not due to
authentic demand. When we provide a **negative** promotion adjustment, we
are telling the forecast system that the PLC would have had higher sales if it
were not for a promotion that was run on another PLC that cannibalized the
former PLC's sales.

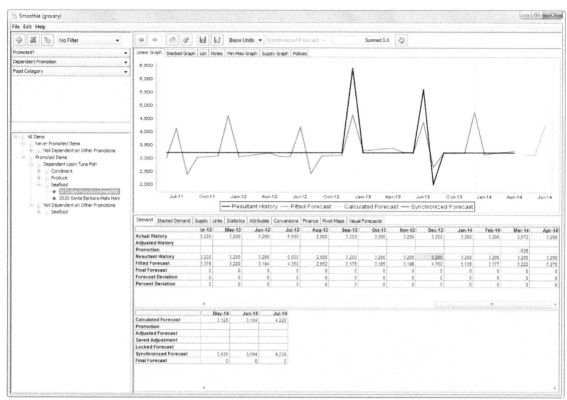

Again in March, we add the value that is calculated by the PAC, which shows that we estimate sales were decreased by 528 units due to the promotion on Tuna Fish, and this increases the Resultant History for Swordfish to 3,200. The Fitted Forecast will use this value rather than the previous value.

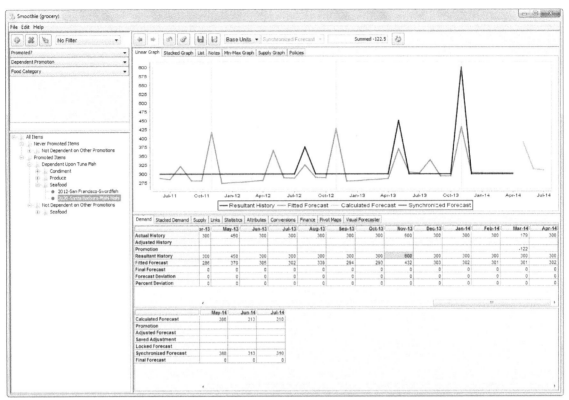

We then make a similar adjustment for Mahi-Mahi. Once all changes are made (to Tuna Fish, Swordfish and Mahi-Mahi), we have neutralized the effect of the promotion on the demand history. We now have a more accurate demand history, which will produce a higher forecast accuracy.

As has been discussed, cannibalization that occurs due to competitor promotions is possible but **much more** difficult to account for in the promotion history. Competitors generally don't like to sit down with you and help you determine their promotion schedule. Thus the promotional activities of competitors make one's own demand history less forecastable. In addition just having companies account for their own promotions would be a big change from how things are currently done at **most** companies. However, if one were to somehow gain access to competitor promotions (most likely by scanning the marketplace and recording the magnitude of the promotion), the process for accounting for these promotions would essentially be the same as the process outlined above. One could build a PAC for competitors' promotions.

Conclusion

As you can see, there are quite a few variations to promotional management for forecasting. It's work, and there is no "magic box" in any forecasting system that can make up for populating the promotion history properly. What is known is that the results of a promotion are more complicated than simply an examination of the immediate effect. Any promotion will of course have an effect on the number of units sold because a reduced price changes the desirability of an item, and while a promotion is often discussed as having only one impact— the initial effect on the number of units sold in the promotional period— it actually has effects in both the short and long term. Promotions must be accounted for in the demand history because they are artificial adjustments to demand.

In this chapter we introduced the concept of the PAC, or Promotion Adjustment Calculator. The PAC estimates the change in demand relative to price changes. When Sales and Marketing provides input to forecasting as to how much a previous month of demand was attributable to a promotion, or how much the forecast should be increased in relation to a promotion, this is really just an informal estimate of what a PAC does more formally. This chapter explained several ways that the PAC can be leveraged to account for promotions.

When promotions are discussed within companies in terms of their impact on forecasting, there is a strong tendency to leave out the "after effects" of promotions. However, the research into promotional effects on demand indicate that it is more likely that some combination of **consumption increase and stockpiling will occur**—and it is likely that it will occur in more than one of the following periods. This chapter used hypothetical examples of how a particular after-effect promotional pattern could be accounted for. Promotions also have a strong tendency to be repeated at certain times of the year, and this produces a faux seasonal pattern that my forecasting system will often pick up when I perform best-fit forecasting analysis for a company.

Many companies believe that inserting their promotional history into their forecasting system is quite onerous, and therefore they don't do it. This is one of the most important misunderstandings to adjust so that a company can manage its promotional history. By doing this, it means much less work over the long term as after promotions are accounted for, forecast accuracy not only improves, but less manual intervention is required in order to achieve a higher forecast accuracy. This chapter provided a very specific set of steps that can be followed by companies in order to achieve this goal.

The types of promotional adjustments to sales history for one particular product location combination are rarely performed in most companies; however, even more rare is accounting for the cannibalization effect of the increase in demand driven by promotions on other product location combinations. And for many companies, however—admittedly, this is a bridge too far—by tracking the history of related product locations, a pattern can be discerned between a specific increased in demand for one product location and a corresponding decrease in demand for another product location. If these patterns can be discerned, they can be acted upon through the same approach described in this book for performing adjustments within one product location combination.

CHAPTER 7

Adding Promotions into the Forecast

This chapter will in some ways seem similar to Chapter 6, "Accounting for Previous Promotions in Sales History," and there are similarities. However, this chapter in fact explains a separate process that adjusts future promotions, rather than past promotion history.

A big part of the process of promotional forecasting is accounting for promotions. This neutralizes the effect of promotions on the history and prevents the forecasting model from either reproducing the promotion quantity change or from increasing the average forecasted quantity. The next step after all promotions (or as many promotions as possible) have been accounted for is to take the future promotions and adjust the forecast. This is done again as part of an interaction between Sales/Marketing and supply chain. The process works in almost the exact same way as in the previous chapter, except now we are adding promotions to the future. Sales/Marketing's input must come to supply chain/forecasting, and then these changes can be made.

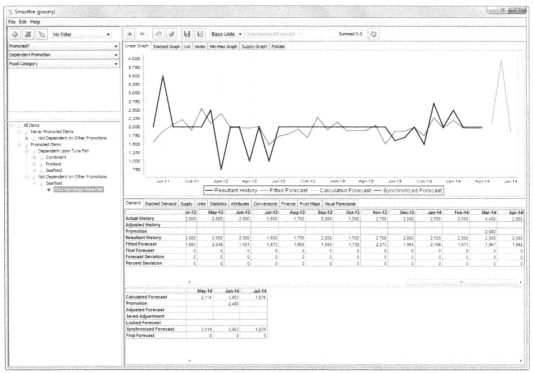

We now make changes to the forecast in anticipation of the future promotion. In this application, the forecasts are shown in the pane below the history pane. Here we add positive promotion adjustment of 2,400 units. This increases the forecast. There is no history to update, because the month has not yet passed. We can see the forecasted increase on the chart as well.

Promotional Adjustment in Aggregate

Recall that we also have two PLC's that are **negatively** correlated with promotions for Tuna Fish; we need to enter negative promotions for those two PLCs for the same month of June. This is a good opportunity to show how promotions can be added in aggregate. In addition to promotional adjustments made to a specific PLC, promotional adjustments can be applied in aggregate, which will allocate the promotion to specific PLCs.

> *"Historic promotions values are automatically deducted from Actual History to produce a baseline forecast. Future promotions are added automatically to the calculated forecast. Promotions can be input on any base-level item, or they may be input on any aggregated node*

(group of items). When inputting promotions on an aggregate node, you will be prompted as to whether you would like the promotions quantities to be allocated to the items in that group. Historic promotions are allocated according to each item's Actual History (unless the promotion value is negative, in which case the Fitted Forecast will be used as the allocation basis), and future promotions are allocated according to each item's Synchronized Forecast. After promotions are allocated, the base level items in that group will be recalculated in order to utilize the new promotions values in the base-level forecast calculations."

– Smoothie Help Documentation

First we select the attribute/hierarchy at the pathway Promoted Items/Dependent Upon Tuna Fish/Negative. This is where PLCs are located that experience lowered sales when Tuna Fish is placed on sale, or have a negative correlation with Tuna Fish promotions. Because both the PLCs within this attribute/hierarchy respond negative-ly, we can add a negative promotion adjustment at the level of the hierarchy and have it percolate down to each PLC. Often this is not useful because in order for it to work,

the PLCs must experience declines that are proportional to their forecast. However, to demonstrate this functionality, let us assume that this is true and insert a decrease of roughly 10 percent of the combined forecast.

When we go to save this change, it asks us if we want to prorate the change made at the attribute/hierarchy, which will allocate the promotion adjustment based upon the forecast for each. We will say yes.

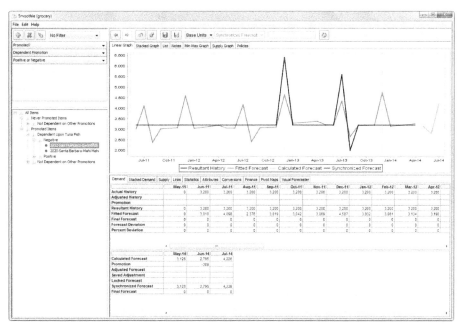

The Swordfish received the majority of the promotion adjustment, because it has the larger forecast.

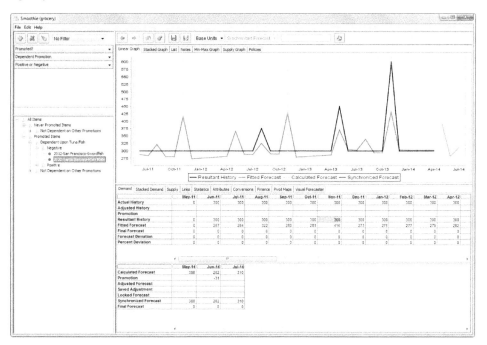

Here is the promotion in units that has been disaggregated to the Mahi-Mahi.

CHAPTER 8

Communicating with Sales/Marketing and the Promotional Adjustment Calculator

It's interesting that many consultants and companies talk about forecast collaboration with supply chain partners, when so many companies don't even collaborate internally. For instance, the communication/collaboration between Sales/Marketing and supply chain on the topic of promotions is, one would assume, a very basic communication channel that would stay open. After all, it is in the self-interest of both entities. Sales/Marketing wants product availability and a higher service level, and supply chain/forecasting wants any information that can cause sales to adjust upwards or downwards; promotions are a prime example of this. In fact, often this is not the case. The demand planners I work with often complain of being blindsided by promotions that were not communicated to them. When the stock invariably runs short of the product, e-mails and calls will frequently come to the demand planner requesting an explanation as to why stock is not available. Quite amazingly, the fact that future promotions must be communicated to forecasting does need to be explained to Sales/Marketing.

How Are Sales and Marketing Inputs Managed?

One major question is whether Sales should go into the system and make the adjustments for promotions to the forecast themselves. This contradicts the experiences I have had working with Sales/Marketing, and the following states my case.

1. *Technical & Quantitative Support:* Sales/Marketing generally **requires** support and guidance in order to translate their domain expertise into good forecasting outcomes. In setting up the forecasting process to simply allow Sales/Marketing to make their adjustments with **little support**, many companies make the error of assuming the marketing intelligence domain expertise of Sales/Marketing with the knowledge of forecasting approaches and forecast adjustment. However, just because a person has market intelligence does not mean that he or she knows how to apply this domain expertise consistently and effectively to forecasting.

2. *Consistency of Input:* Sales/Marketing is known to periodically forget to update the forecast. I have yet to work with a sales or marketing group that actually preferred to provide forecasting input over doing the core parts of their jobs. And as with anything, if a person does not like doing something, they often do it inconsistently. Meeting with Sales/Marketing to go over promotions and other adjustments puts it on their calendars and makes it something that has to be done.

Incentives are another important consideration. In most cases, Sales/Marketing does not have service levels or forecast accuracy as part of its yearly performance ratings, and if it does, they are weighed very lightly when compared to the criteria of sales. This seems to be a major point of confusion in many companies, where individuals outside of sales and marketing try to get sales and marketing to focus on forecast accuracy. However, even the VPs of Sales or Marketing are not measured to much degree on forecast accuracy or service level, so why would those who work for them be measured this way, or value service level or forecast accuracy over sales?

The Supply Chain department has a greater incentive to get the future promotional adjustments into the system than Sales/Marketing. Firstly, they are measured on service levels and forecast accuracy. Secondly, when the stock-out occurs in the month of the promotion, the stock-out tends to quickly become the primary focus; the fact that the PLC was on promotion (and possibly the information was not communicated to Supply Chain, or was communicated late to Supply Chain) seems to recede into the background. An executive once asked me about a stock-out and I informed him of the fact it was due to a promotion that had not been communicated to Forecasting. The response I received was, *"I don't want to talk about the past right now; I want to talk about what we are going to do about fixing the problem."* In this case, and in several other cases, the Supply Chain department tends to get dinged more than the Sales/Marketing department.

There are really three steps required to implement promotion forecast adjustments.

1. *Obtain Sales/Marketing Information on Promotions*: Obviously, it's necessary to find out from Sales/Marketing the upcoming promotions, as well as the price changes per promotion.

2. *Build/Use the Promotion Adjustment Calculator*: In order to make any adjustment to the forecast (through the promotions row), it is necessary to know what the expected change in volume will be. This is typically stated in terms of the change in volume per 1 percent change in the price of the item. The PAC is created during the process of accounting for the promotional effect in sales history.

3. *Make the Adjustments within the Forecasting System*: This was covered in Chapter 7, "Adding Promotions into the Forecast."

Step 1—Obtain Sales/Marketing Information on Promotions

This is a matter of Sales/Marketing making the communication of future promotions a priority and of the supply chain-planning department working with Sales/Marketing to develop an easy way for them to provide the data that forecasting needs. Currently, in quite a few companies, promotions are communicated by e-mail to Supply Chain. The individual promotions are communicated in individual e-mails, such as the following:

From: John Smith
To: Patti Cake

Subject: New Promotion

Patti,

This is just to let you know that we have decided to put product 54326 on promotion in August. We will be offering a 10 percent price decrease.

Regards,

John Smith
Account Manager – Produce

When Patti wants to see the overall promotions she needs to account for, if she has not recorded them in a separate document, she needs to go through her e-mail searching for the term "promotions." The subject of the e-mail may be titled "incentives," or a different term may have been used, so there is no guarantee that Patti will see all promotions. Overall this is not a good way of communicating promotional changes.

Sales/Marketing does not just put a product on promotion at the spur of the moment. They have a promotion plan or calendar. There is no reason this plan can't be shared and discussed with Supply Chain. Something like the following is all that is necessary.

Promotion Plan

Product Category	Product	Price Reduction Per Product Per Month			
		Jan	Feb	March	April
A	Tuna Fish	15%	0%	0%	0%
A	Swordfish	0%	18%	0%	0%
A	Mahi Mahi	0%	0%	0%	12%

Here we have included the promotion schedule into the future, which we received from Sales/Marketing. The promotion schedule adjusts the forecast. It contains is the price change along with the month and the product. This promotion plan should be sent to the forecasting group, and then it should be the primary discussion document during Sales/Marketing and forecasting meetings.

Step 2—Build/Use the Promotion Adjustment Calculator

The PAC is developed through previous volume changes based upon previous price changes. Typically (or at least quite often) the company will not have this information except in some specialized system. That is why I recommend building the PAC through the process described in Chapter 7, "Adding Promotions into the Forecast." However, once the PAC is complete we can begin using it for the following types of adjustments.

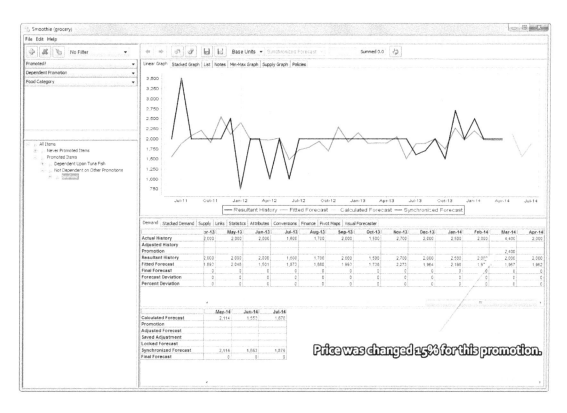

In addition to obtaining the estimate of the size of the promotional effect, it is necessary to find out the size of price change for each promotion. This results in the creation of a promotion database, which can then be used to create the PAC.

Price to Volume Observations

Product Category	Product	Per Product Per Observation			
		Observation 1	Observation 2	Observation 3	Observation 4
A	Tuna Fish Price Change	15%	10%	7%	16%
A	Tuna Fish Sales Volume Change Per Percentage Point of Change in Price	8%	3%	2%	6%

Average Change in Volume Per Percentage Point Change in Price	5%

This list of observations can be used to create an average, which can then be applied to future promotions. In this case, there is variability in the relationship between the price change and the change in the volume sold, based upon the particular observation. However, the average is 5 percent. The company does not have to use a straight average; it may have some extra insight that would cause it to weigh some of the observations more heavily than others.

One of the issues with creating a database of this type is that more observations tend to provide a more accurate number. However, the more specific the calculation—that is, if it is made for the PLC—there will be fewer observations. Let's take the example of Hothouse Tomatoes. The company only has two previous promotions by which to determine the relationship.

Price to Volume Observations

Product Category	Product	Per Product Per Observation			
		Observation 1	Observation 2	Observation 3	Observation 4
C	Hothouse Tomatoes Price Change	15%	20%		
C	Hothouse Tomatoes Sales Volume Change Per Percentage Point of Change in Price	2%	6%		

Average Change in Volume Per Percentage Point Change in Price	4%

We could use the average of 4 percent, but there is a very large difference between the increases in sales between the two observations. There is, as would be expected, a larger

*increase in sales from the large price reduction. However, promotions also have vari-ability; the same price decrease will not result in the same increase in sales volume. At this point a company may consider if a PAC should be created for a **group of prod-ucts**. For instance, it's reasonable to think that the effect of price reductions on Hot-house Tomatoes would be similar to other varieties of tomatoes offered by the company. By creating a group PAC, more data points can be brought into the fold.*

Price to Volume Observations

Product Category	Product	Per Product Per Observation			
		Observation 1	Observation 2	Observation 3	Observation 4
C	Hothouse Tomatoes Price Change	15%	20%		
C	Hothouse Tomatoes Sales Volume Change Per Percentage Point of Change in Price	2%	6%		
C	Beefsteak Tomatoes Price Change	10%	15%	20%	
C	Beefsteak Tomatoes Sales Volume Change Per Percentage Point of Change in Price	2%	3%	4%	

Average Change in Volume Per Percentage Point Change in Price	3%

From these extra observations, it appears that the volume change for Beefsteak Toma-toes is closer to the first observation for hothouse tomatoes than the second observation for Hothouse Tomatoes. There is no perfect answer here, because we are assuming that different varieties of tomatoes respond in a similar manner to price changes. However, when analysis of this type is performed, patterns become clearer regarding the interac-tion between promotions and volume changes.

Free Sample to Volume Observations

Product Category	Product	Per Product Per Observation			
		Observation 1	Observation 2	Observation 3	Observation 4
C	Hothouse Tomatoes Free Samples Offered at X Percentage of Stores	30%	50%		
C	Hothouse Tomatoes Sales Volume Change	40%	25%		
C	Beefsteak Tomatoes at X Percentage of Stores	20%	50%	20%	
C	Beefsteak Tomatoes Sales Volume Change	30%	55%	35%	

Average Change in Volume Per Promotion Program	37%

As was pointed out in Chapter 1, "Introduction," many different types of promotions can be run. However, this same approach applies to any type of promotion. The table above records the change in sales due to the promotion of giving away free samples at a store. The promotion is run for different percentages of the stores in most cases, and has a different impact on the sales of the beefsteak tomatoes. Any type of promotion can be recorded this way, and the relationship then used to adjust the forecast.

So far we have only shown a few examples of products. However, as the company builds up its database of promotion changes for many products, it can begin to see patterns, calculate averages for groups of similar products, and use the PAC to create estimated promotional forecast adjustments for never-before promoted products.

Step 3—Make the Adjustments within the Forecasting System

With this step, we simply perform what was described in Chapter 7. This is actually the easiest step of the process. As was explained in Chapter 7, it's quite likely that the company's current forecasting system is not the best system in which to make these adjustments. However, Adjusted/Resultant History can be easily exported from the forecast adjustment system and then uploaded to the forecasting system.

Conclusion

Promotional forecasting is not a major emphasis of forecasting books, forecasting classes or statistical forecasting. However, promotions can be an incredibly powerful influence on the demand and a major factor in reducing forecast accuracy when unaccounted for in the demand history. Promotions degrade forecast accuracy by increasing the variability of the sales history, creating unexpected spikes in demand, and increasing the work on the part of the demand planner, as well as on the part of many other individuals throughout the supply chain. While this may not seem like a major problem, companies generally greatly **understaff** the forecasting area. Therefore, every extra overhead with respect to forecasting tends to lessen the likelihood that the item in question will be accounted for. At many companies, promotions are a primary focus of Sales/Marketing and the use of promotions has grown very rapidly, along with the proportion of company revenues that they consume. The literature from Marketing on promotions (which is the vast majority of literature that is written on the topic) seems to deliberately leave out many of the costs related to promotions. Executives outside of marketing are far too complacent in accepting the universal benefits of promotions that are most frequently presented by

Marketing—and often Sales—as to why a high level of promotions is good for the company. Many non-marketing executives assume that as promotions are the domain expertise of those in marketing, the marketers must know what they are talking about. However, what these non-marketing executives do not account for is that both Sales and Marketing have a bias in their use of promotions. By oversimplifying how promotions actually work to impact the demand of a company, and by minimizing the costs of running promotions, Sales and Marketing are able to make their contribution to the company seem larger than they actually are. This is, in my view, why the presentation of the topic of promotions by both Sales and Marketing is inconsistent with the published research on promotions. Because of this, many companies that run promotions do so reflexively because promotions are supposed to increase sales; however, because they generally don't pay attention to the research on promotions, they are not cognizant of how promotions are run. As a result, many companies are running mindless promotions that contribute little to profitability. Both Sales and Marketing have a very parochial view of what a company should be striving towards. Because of their incentives, both Sales and Marketing are highly biased towards maximizing revenue; however, the company is actually supposed to be maximizing profit. This is the point made by the book *Islands of Profit in a Sea of Red Ink*.

This is explained by the following quotation:

> *"Nearly every company is 30 t0 40 percent unprofitable by any measure. In almost every company 20 to 30 percent of the business is highly profitable, and a large proportion of this profitability is going to cross-subsidize the unprofitable part of the business. The rest of the company is marginal. The most current metrics and control systems (budgets, etc.) do not even show the problem or the opportunity for improvement."*

This is the problem: when you create incentives for groups that are entirely focused on maximizing sales, it is quite predictable that the company will metastasize into areas that are not profitable.

Many companies believe that inserting their promotional history into their forecasting system is quite onerous, and therefore they don't do it. This is one of the most important misunderstandings to adjust so that a company can manage its promotional history. By doing this, it means much less work over the long term as after promotions are accounted for, forecast accuracy not only improves, but less manual intervention is required in order to achieve a higher forecast accuracy. This chapter provided a very specific set of steps that can be followed by companies in order to achieve this goal.

Promotional adjustments to sales history for one particular product location combination are rarely performed in most companies; even more rare is accounting for the cannibalization effect of the increase in demand, driven by promotions, on other product location combinations. However, this is not nearly as complex or time-consuming as most companies assume. It requires input from Marketing in order to build the Promotion Adjustment Calculator, and it requires the right forecasting system (most often not simply the forecasting system that the company already has) in order to make the adjustments once the relationship is apparent from the Promotion Adjustment Calculator. However, the use of a small and easy-to-use forecasting system for adjusting sales history does not mean that the currently used forecasting system needs to be replaced. This is another major area of misunderstanding on the part of many companies—that only a single statistical forecasting system should be used, or that the use of other forecasting systems in conjunction with the main production forecasting system is expensive or complicated.

A major component to the method laid out in this book is the close interaction between the forecasting group (out of supply chain) and Sales and Marketing. This does not mean more time spent by Sales or Marketing; in fact, it means less. Following this method will mean systematizing the marketing intelligence from Sales and Marketing so that the statistical forecasting system actually requires less input from Sales and Marketing and less input overall in the form of manual adjustments. A number of forecasting books have made the point quite well, and explained that the research conclusion from quite a few studies is that far too many manual adjustments are performed. However, companies by and large are ignoring this research and reducing their forecast accuracy by continuing to allow for high numbers of manual forecast adjustments. At least one of the reasons why this continues to be the case is that so many basic areas of forecasting are not properly leveraged within companies, and this leads to the impression that manual adjustments can account for these unpredictable factors.

This book explains that promotions must both be accounted for in sales history as well adjusted into the forecast. Communication is critical in both areas. However, the communication on future promotions as a tendency to be poor. Being blindsided by promotions that were not communicated to supply chain is a common issue. Quite amazingly, the fact that future promotions must be communicated to forecasting does need to be explained to Sales/Marketing.

My experience has lead me to conclude that there are significant opportunities for improving the management of promotion forecasting. Promotions management does not require a new fancy approach, but does require following a disciplined process. It requires an understanding of the relationship between the event or promotion and the change in demand, and the right tools for incorporating this relationship into sales history and forecasts. For companies have a sizable number of promotions, it is extremely important that the effect of promotions on sales be managed. I also see no reason that it cannot be.

References

Ailawadi, Kusum L., Karen Gedenk, Christian Lutzky, and Scott A. Neslin. *Decomposition of the Sales Impact of Promotion-Induced Stockpiling.* AMA Publishing. http://www.marketingpower.com/AboutAMA/Pages/AMA%20Publications/AMA%20Journals/Journal%20of%20Marketing%20Research/TOCs/summary%20aug%2007/Decompositionjmraug07.aspx.

Anderson, George. *Why Are Trader Joe's Customers The Most Satisfied In America?* Forbes. July 30, 2014. http://www.forbes.com/sites/retailwire/2013/07/30/why-are-trader-joes-customers-the-most-satisfied-in-america/.

Black Box. Accessed May 4, 2014. http://en.wikipedia.org/wiki/Black_box.

Byrnes, Jonathan. Islands of Profit in a Sea of Red Ink. Portfolio Hardcover. 2010.

Centralization: The New Promotion Paradigm. July 2013. http://www.retalix.com/data/product_pdf/RET_CentralizationWhitePaper3.pdf.

David, John P. *Catastrophic Success at Trader Joe's*. Huffington Post. October 31, 2013.
http://www.huffingtonpost.com/john-p-david/catastrophic-success-at-trader-joes_b_4181699.html.

Demand Planning and Forecasting.
http://help.sap.com/SCENARIOS_BUS2008/helpdata/EN/49/ed4c6eefc923d3e10000000a42189b/content.htm.

Demand Works Smoothie Help Documentation. Demand Works. Version 7.3: 2013.

Donnelly, Tim. *How to Start a Customer Rewards Program*. Inc. August 17, 2010.
http://www.inc.com/guides/2010/08/how-to-start-a-customer-rewards-program.html.

Enderle, Rob. *How Oracle Is Giving Up Account Control to IBM*. IT Business Edge. October 3, 2011.
http://www.itbusinessedge.com/cm/blogs/enderle/how-oracle-is-giving-up-account-control-to-ibm/?cs=48755.

Forecasting—Automatic Model Selection using Process 2. November 13, 2008.
http://www.sapfans.com/forums/viewtopic.php?f=6&t=321091.

Ozden, Gur Ali, Serpil Sayin, Tom Van Woensel, and Jan Fransoo. *SKU Demand Forecasting in the Presence of Promotions*. Expert Systems with Applications. Vol 36: December 1, 2009.

Hagemeyer, Dale. *Vendor Panorama for Trade Promotion Management in Consumer Goods*. Gartner. August 31, 2012.

John Maynard Keynes. Accessed May 13, 2014.
https://en.wikipedia.org/wiki/John_Maynard_Keynes.

Kanagasabapathi, Balasubramanian, Shoban B. Babu, and Mitul Shah. *Forecasting Volumes for Trade Promotions in CPG Industry Using Market Drivers*. International Journal of Business Forecasting and Market Intelligence. November 2009.

Lapide, Larry. *Demand Shaping with Supply in Mind*. Supply Chain 247. December 09, 2013.

Lucas, Anthony. *In-Store Trade Promotions – Profit or Loss?* Journal of Consumer Marketing. April 1, 1996.

Manna, Somnath. *Why to Choose APO over R/3 for Planning*. May 14, 2007. http://scn.sap.com/thread/406157.

Mello, John E. *Sales Forecast "Game Playing" - Why It's Bad and What You Can Do About It*. Arkansas State University. http://forecasters.org/foresight/wp/wp-content/uploads/Forecast_Game_Playing_ Mello_OSU_IIF_13.pdf.

Method and System for Demand Modeling and Demand Forecasting Promotional Tactics. US Patent Office Abstracts. Patent Number 20130066678. March 14, 2013.

Metzer, John. T., and Carol. C. Dienstock. *Sales Forecasting Management*. Sage Publications, 1998.

Overfitting. Accessed April, 20 2014. https://en.wikipedia.org/wiki/Overfitting.

Sales Promotions. Accessed May 5, 2014. https://en.wikipedia.org/wiki/Sales_promotion.

SAS Revenue Optimization Suite. http://www.sas.com/en_us/industry/retail/revenue-optimization.html.

Sievers, David, Hanna Hamburger, and Julie Bonne. *Uncovering the Hidden Costs of Trade Promotions*. Sales and Marketing Management, July 31, 2010. http://www.salesandmarketing.com/article/uncovering-hidden-costs-trade-promotions.

Snapp, Shaun. *Cost vs. Duration Based Optimization for Production Scheduling*. January 20, 2011.

http://www.scmfocus.com/productionplanningandscheduling/2011/01/20/cost-vs-duration-based-optimization-for-scheduling/.

Snapp, Shaun. *Customizing the Optimization Per Supply Chain Domain.* July 10, 2011.
http://www.scmfocus.com/supplyplanning/2011/07/10/customizing-the-optimization-per-supply-chain-domain/.

Snapp, Shaun. *How Far is a Solution from the Optimal?* September 26, 2011.
http://www.scmfocus.com/supplychainsimulation/2011/09/26/how-far-is-a-solution-from-the-optimal/.

Snapp, Shaun. *Supply Chain Forecasting Software.* SCM Focus Press, 2012.

Snapp Shaun. *The Bill of Materials in Excel, Planning, ERP and BMMS/PLM Software.* SCM Focus Press, 2012

Snapp, Shaun. *The Real Story Behind ERP: Separating Fiction from Reality.* SCM Focus Press, 2013.

Srinivasan, Shuba, Koen Pauwels, Dominique Hanssens, and Marnik Dekimpe. *Who Benefits from Price Promotions.* Harvard Business Review. September 2002.

Speizer, Irwin. *The Grocery Chain That Shouldn't Be.* Fast Company. February 2004.
http://www.fastcompany.com/48666/grocery-chain-shouldnt-be.

Su, Xuanming. *Intemporal Pricing and Consumer Stockpiling.* Operations Research. July –August, 2010.
http://www.deepdyve.com/lp/informs/intertemporal-pricing-and-consumer-stockpiling-iFZB38Ikz1?articleList=%2Fsearch%3Fquery%3Dstockpiling%2Bpromotions.

Tokar, Travis, John A. Aloysisus, Matthew A. Waller, and Brent D. Williams. *Retail Promotions and Information Sharing in the Supply Chain: A Controlled Experiment.* The International Journal of Logistics Management. Vol 22, No 1: 2011.

Trader Joe's FAQ.
http://www.traderjoes.com/about/general-faq.asp.

Trader Joe's: The Forgotten Supermarket Giant. June 10, 2007.
http://www.brandautopsy.com/2007/06/trader_joes_the_1.html.

Trader Joe's vs. Whole Foods Market: A Comparison of Operational Management.
MIT Sloan School of Management.
http://ocw.mit.edu/courses/sloan-school-of-management/15-768-management-of-services-concepts-design-and-delivery-fall-2010/projects/MIT15_768F10_paper05.pdf.

Vermorel, Joannes. *Better Promotion Forecasts in Retail.* April 3, 2009.
http://blog.lokad.com/journal/2009/4/3/better-promotion-forecasts-in-retail.html.

Vermorel, Joannes. *Overfitting: When Accuracy Measure Goes Wrong.* April 22, 2009.
http://blog.lokad.com/journal/2009/4/22/overfitting-when-accuracy-measure-goes-wrong.html

Other books from SCM Focus

Vendor Acknowledgments and Profiles

I have listed brief profiles of each vendor with screen shots included in this book below.

Profiles:

Demand Works
Demand Works is a best-of-breed demand-and-supply-planning vendor that emphasizes flexible and easy-to-configure solutions. This book only focuses on the supply planning functionality within their Smoothie product, which includes MRP and DRP.

http://www.demandworks.com

JDA
JDA was started in 1978 and offers a wide variety of supply chain applications.

JDA has thirty-seven offices with 3,000 employees and is a combination of brands including i2 Technologies, Manugistics, E3, Intactix and Arthur Retail.

http://www.jda.com

SAP

SAP does not need much of an introduction. They are the largest vendor of enterprise software applications for supply chain management. SAP has multiple products that are showcased in this book, including SAP ERP and SAP APO.

www.sap.com

ToolsGroup

ToolsGroup offers unique probability-based supply chain planning (SCP) and inventory optimization solutions that allow companies to master even large, heterogeneous, or demanding supply chains. On the demand side, they incorporate best-of-breed demand modeling, order frequency forecasting, and demand-sensing technology. On the supply side, they offer multi-echelon inventory optimization and replenishment planning.

http://www.toolsgroup.com

Author Profile

Shaun Snapp is the founder and editor of SCM Focus. SCM Focus is one of the largest independent supply chain software analysis and educational sites on the Internet.

After working at several of the largest consulting companies and at i2 Technologies, he became an independent consultant and later started SCM Focus. He maintains a strong interest in comparative software design, and works both in SAP APO as well as with a variety of best-of-breed supply chain planning vendors. His ongoing relationships with these vendors keep him on the cutting edge of emerging technology.

Primary Sources of Information and Writing Topics
Shaun writes about topics with which he has firsthand experience. These topics range from recovering problematic implementations, to system configuration, to socializing complex software and supply chain concepts in the areas of demand planning, supply planning and production planning.

More broadly, he writes on topics supportive of these applications, which include master data parameter management, integration, analytics, simulation and bill of material management systems. He covers management aspects of enterprise software ranging from software policy to handling consulting partners on SAP projects.

Shaun writes from an implementer's perspective and as a result he focuses on how software is actually used in practice rather than its hypothetical or "pure release note capabilities." Unlike many authors in enterprise software who keep their distance from discussing the realities of software implementation, he writes both on the problems as well as the successes of his software use. This gives him a distinctive voice in the field.

Secondary Sources of Information

In addition to project experience, Shaun's interest in academic literature is a secondary source of information for his books and articles. Intrigued with the historical perspective of supply chain software, much of his writing is influenced by his readings and research into how different categories of supply chain software developed, evolved, and finally became broadly used over time.

Covering the Latest Software Developments

Shaun is focused on supply chain software selections and implementation improvement through writing and consulting, bringing companies some of the newest technologies and methods. Some of the software developments that Shaun showcases at SCM Focus and in books at SCM Focus Press have yet to reach widespread adoption.

Education

Shaun has an undergraduate degree in business from the University of Hawaii, a Master of Science in Maritime Management from the Maine Maritime Academy and a Master of Science in Business Logistics from Penn State University. He has taught both logistics and SAP software.

Software Certifications

Shaun has been trained and/or certified in products from i2 Technologies, Servigistics, ToolsGroup and SAP (SD, DP, SNP, SPP, EWM).

Contact

Shaun can be contacted at:
shaunsnapp@scmfocus.com
www.scmfocus.com

Abbreviations

APO – Advanced Planning and Optimizer

CPG – Consumer Package Goods

ERP – Enterprise Resource Planning

MAPE – Mean Absolute Percentage Error

PLC – Product Location Combination

RMSE – Root Mean Square Error

ROI – Return on Investment

SKU – Stock Keeping Unit

Links Listed in the Book by Chapter

Chapter 1:

http://www.scmfocus.com/scmfocuspress/promotions-forecasting/

Chapter 5:

http://www.scmfocus.com/fourthpartylogistics/

http://www.scmfocus.com/demandplanning/2010/07/crostons-vs-smoothie-methods/

http://www.scmfocus.com/demandplanning/2010/06/forecastable-non-fore-castable-formula/

Chapter 6:

http://www.softwaredecisions.org

www.ingramcontent.com/pod-product-compliance
Lightning Source LLC
LaVergne TN
LVHW080059070326
832902LV00014B/2314